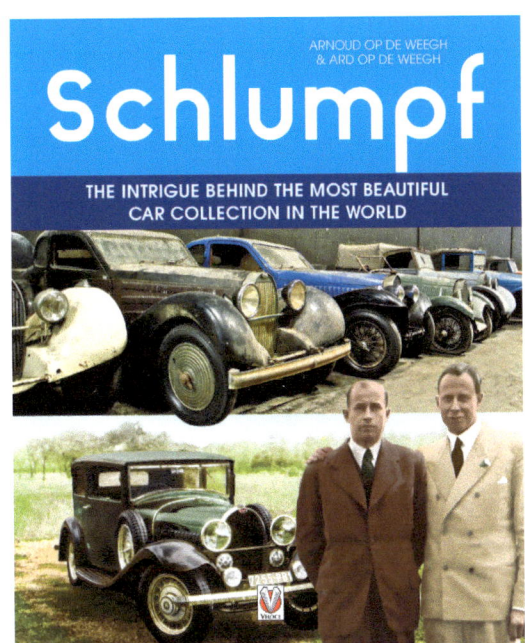

Great Cars
Austin-Healey – A celebration of the fabulous 'Big' Healey (Piggott)
Jaguar E-type (Thorley)
Jaguar Mark 1 & 2 (Thorley)
Triumph TR – TR2 to 6: The last of the traditional sports cars (Piggott)

Biographies
A Chequered Life – Graham Warner and the Chequered Flag (Hesletine)
A Life Awheel – The 'auto' biography of W de Forte (Skelton)
Amédée Gordini ... a true racing legend (Smith)
André Lefebvre, and the cars he created at Voisin and Citroën (Beck)
Chris Carter at Large – Stories from a lifetime in motorcycle racing (Carter & Skelton)
Cliff Allison, The Official Biography of – From the Fells to Ferrari (Gauld)
Driven by Desire – The Desiré Wilson Story
First Principles – The Official Biography of Keith Duckworth (Burr)
Inspired to Design – F1 cars, Indycars & racing tyres: the autobiography of Nigel Bennett (Bennett)
Jack Sears, The Official Biography of – Gentleman Jack (Gauld)
John Chatham – 'Mr Big Healey' – The Official Biography (Burr)
The Lee Noble Story (Wilkins)
Mason's Motoring Mayhem – Tony Mason's hectic life in motorsport and television (Mason)
Raymond Mays' Magnificent Obsession (Apps)
Pat Moss Carlsson Story, The – Harnessing Horsepower (Turner)
Tony Robinson – The biography of a race mechanic (Wagstaff)
Virgil Exner – Visioneer: The Official Biography of Virgil M Exner Designer Extraordinaire (Grist)

General
1½-litre GP Racing 1961-1965 (Whitelock)
AC Two-litre Saloons & Buckland Sportscars (Archibald)
Alfa Romeo 155/156/147 Competition Touring Cars (Collins)
Alfa Romeo Giulia Coupé GT & GTA (Tipler)
Alfa Romeo Montreal – The dream car that came true (Taylor)
Alfa Romeo Montreal – The Essential Companion (Classic Reprint of 500 copies) (Taylor)
Alfa Tipo 33 (McDonough & Collins)
Alpine & Renault – The Development of the Revolutionary Turbo F1 Car 1968 to 1979 (Smith)
Alpine & Renault – The Sports Prototypes 1963 to 1969 (Smith)
Alpine & Renault – The Sports Prototypes 1973 to 1978 (Smith)
An Austin Anthology (Stringer)
An Incredible Journey (Falls & Reisch)
Anatomy of the Classic Mini (Huthert & Ely)
Anatomy of the Works Minis (Moylan)
Armstrong-Siddeley (Smith)
Art Deco and British Car Design (Down)
Austin Cars 1948 to 1990 – a pictorial history (Rowe)
Autodrome (Collins & Ireland)
Automotive A-Z, Lane's Dictionary of Automotive Terms (Lane)
Automotive Mascots (Kay & Springate)
Bahamas Speed Weeks, The (O'Neil)
Bentley Continental, Corniche and Azure (Bennett)
Bentley MkVI, Rolls-Royce Silver Wraith, Dawn & Cloud/Bentley R & S-Series (Nutland)
Bluebird CN7 (Stevens)
BMC Competitions Department Secrets (Turner, Chambers & Browning)
BMW 5-Series (Cranswick)
BMW Z-Cars (Taylor)
BMW Classic 5 Series 1972 to 2003 (Cranswick)
BMW – The Power of M (Vivian)
British at Indianapolis, The (Wagstaff)
British Cars, The Complete Catalogue of, 1895-1975 (Culshaw & Horrobin)
BRM – A Mechanic's Tale (Salmon)
BRM V16 (Ludvigsen)
Bugatti – The 8-cylinder Touring Cars 1920-34 (Price & Arbey)
Bugatti Type 40 (Price)
Bugatti 46/50 Updated Edition (Price & Arbey)
Bugatti T44 & T49 (Price & Arbey)
Bugatti 57 2nd Edition (Price)
Bugatti Type 57 Grand Prix – A Celebration (Tomlinson)
Carrera Panamericana, La (Tipler)
Car-tastrophes – 80 automotive atrocities from the past 20 years (Honest John, Fowler)
Chrysler 300 – America's Most Powerful Car 2nd Edition (Ackerson)
Chrysler PT Cruiser (Ackerson)
Citroën DS (Bobbitt)
Cobra – The Real Thing! (Legate)
Concept Cars, How to illustrate and design – New 2nd Edition (Dewey)
Cortina – Ford's Bestseller (Robson)
Cosworth – The Search for Power (6th edition) (Robson)
Coventry Climax Racing Engines (Hammill)
Daily Mirror 1970 World Cup Rally 40, The (Robson)
Daimler SP250 New Edition (Long)
Datsun Fairlady Roadster to 280ZX – The Z-Car Story (Long)
Dino – The V6 Ferrari (Long)
Dodge Challenger & Plymouth Barracuda (Grist)
Dodge Charger – Enduring Thunder (Ackerson)
Dodge Dynamite! (Grist)
Draw & Paint Cars – How to (Gardiner)
Drive on the Wild Side, A – 20 Extreme Driving Adventures From Around the World (Weaver)
East German Motor Vehicles in Pictures (Suhr/Weinreich)
Essential Guide to Driving in Europe, The (Parish)
Fast Ladies – Female Racing Drivers 1888 to 1970 (Bouzanquet)
Fate of the Sleeping Beauties, The (op de Weegh/Hottendorff/op de Weegh)
Ferrari 288 GTO, The Book of the (Sackey)
Ferrari 333 SP (O'Neil)
Fiat & Abarth 124 Spider & Coupé (Tipler)
Fiat & Abarth 500 & 600 – 2nd Edition (Bobbitt)
Fiats, Great Small (Ward)
Ford Cleveland 335-Series V8 engine 1970 to 1982 – The Essential Source Book (Hammill)
Ford F100/F150 Pick-up 1948-1996 (Ackerson)
Ford F150 Pick-up 1997-2005 (Ackerson)
Ford Focus WRC (Robson)
Ford GT – Then, and Now (Streather)
Ford GT40 (Legate)
Ford Midsize Muscle – Fairlane, Torino & Ranchero (Cranswick)
Ford Model Y (Roberts)
Ford Small Block V8 Racing Engines 1962-1970 – The Essential Source Book (Hammill)
Ford Thunderbird From 1954, The Book of the (Long)
Formula One – The Real Score? (Harvey)
Formula 5000 Motor Racing, Back then ... and back now (Lawson)
Forza Minardi! (Vigar)
France: the essential guide for car enthusiasts – 200 things for the car enthusiast to see and do (Parish)
Franklin's Indians (Sucher/Pickering/Diamond/Havelin)
The Good, the Mad and the Ugly ... not to mention Jeremy Clarkson (Dron)
Grand Prix Ferrari – The Years of Enzo Ferrari's Power, 1948-1980 (Pritchard)
Grand Prix Ford – DFV-powered Formula 1 Cars (Robson)
GT – The World's Best GT Cars 1953-73 (Dawson)
Hillclimbing & Sprinting – The Essential Manual (Short & Wilkinson)
Honda NSX (Long)
Immortal Austin Seven (Morgan)
Inside the Rolls-Royce & Bentley Styling Department – 1971 to 2001 (Hull)
Intermeccanica – The Story of the Prancing Bull (McCredie & Reisner)
Jaguar from the shop floor (Martin)
Jaguar E-type Factory and Private Competition Cars (Griffiths)
Jaguar, The Rise of (Price)
Jaguar XJ 220 – The Inside Story (Moreton)
Jaguar XJ-S, The Book of the (Long)
Jeep CJ (Ackerson)
Jeep Wrangler (Ackerson)
The Jowett Jupiter – The car that leaped to fame (Nankivell)
Karmann-Ghia Coupé & Convertible (Bobbitt)
Kris Meeke – Intercontinental Rally Challenge Champion (McBride)
Lamborghini Miura Bible, The (Sackey)
Lamborghini Murciélago, The book of the (Pathmanathan)
Lamborghini Urraco, The Book of the (Landsem)
Lancia 037 (Collins)
Lancia Delta HF Integrale (Blaettel & Wagner)
Lancia Delta Integrale (Collins)
Land Rover Emergency Vehicles (Taylor)
Land Rover Series III Reborn (Porter)
Land Rover, The Half-ton Military (Cook)
Land Rovers in British Military Service – coil sprung models 1970 to 2007 (Taylor)
Lea-Francis Story, The (Price)
Le Mans Panoramic (Ireland)
Lexus Story, The (Long)
Little book of microcars, the (Quellin)
Little book of smart, the – New Edition (Jackson)
Little book of trikes, the (Quellin)
Lola – The Illustrated History (1957-1977) (Starkey)
Lola – All the Sports Racing & Single-seater Racing Cars 1978-1997 (Starkey)
Lola T70 – The Racing History & Individual Chassis Record – 4th Edition (Starkey)
Lotus 18 Colin Chapman's U-turn (Whitelock)
Lotus 49 (Oliver)
Maserati 250F In Focus (Pritchard)
Mazda MX-5 Miata, The book of the – The 'Mk1' NA-series 1988 to 1997 (Long)
Mazda MX-5 Miata, The book of the – The 'Mk2' NB-series 1997 to 2004 (Long)
Mazda MX-5 Miata Roadster (Long)
Mazda Rotary-engined Cars (Cranswick)
Maximum Mini (Booij)
Mercedes-Benz SL – R230 series 2001 to 2011 (Long)
Mercedes-Benz SL – W113-series 1963-1971 (Long)
Mercedes-Benz SL & SLC – 107-series 1971-1989 (Long)
Mercedes-Benz SLK – R170 series 1996-2004 (Long)
Mercedes-Benz SLK – R171 series 2004-2011 (Long)
Mercedes-Benz W123-series – All models 1976 to 1986 (Long)
Mercedes G-Wagen (Long)
MG, Made in Abingdon (Frampton)
MGA (Price Williams)
MGB & MGB GT– Expert Guide (Auto-doc Series) (Williams)
MGB Electrical Systems Updated & Revised Edition (Astley)
Mini Cooper – The Real Thing! (Tipler)
Mini Minor to Asia Minor (West)
Mitsubishi Lancer Evo, The Road Car & WRC Story (Long)
Montlhéry, The Story of the Paris Autodrome (Boddy)
MOPAR Muscle – Barracuda, Dart & Valiant 1960-1980 (Cranswick)
Morgan Maverick (Lawrence)
Morgan 3 Wheeler – back to the future!, The (Dron)
Morris Minor, 70 Years on the Road (Newell)
Motor Racing – Reflections of a Lost Era (Carter)
Motor Racing – The Pursuit of Victory 1930-1962 (Carter)
Motor Racing – The Pursuit of Victory 1963-1972 (Wyatt/Sears)
Motor Racing Heroes – The Stories of 100 Greats (Newman)
Motorcycle Apprentice (Cakebread)
Motorcycling in the '50s (Clew)
Motorsport In colour, 1950s (Wainwright)
N.A.R.T. – A concise history of the North American Racing Team 1957 to 1983 (O'Neil)
Nissan 300ZX & 350Z – The Z-Car Story (Long)
Nissan GT-R Supercar: Born to race (Gorodji)
Northeast American Sports Car Races 1950-1959 (O'Neil)
Nothing Runs – Misadventures in the Classic, Collectable & Exotic Car Biz (Slutsky)
Pass the Theory and Practical Driving Tests (Gibson & Hoole)
Peking to Paris 2007 (Young)
Pontiac Firebird – New 3rd Edition (Cranswick)
Porsche 356 (2nd Edition) (Long)
Porsche 908 (Födisch, Neßhöver, Roßbach, Schwarz & Roßbach)
Porsche 911 Carrera – The Last of the Evolution (Corlett)
Porsche 911R, RS & RSR, 4th Edition (Starkey)
Porsche 911, The Book of the (Long)
Porsche 911 – The Definitive History 2004-2012 (Long)
Porsche – The Racing 914s (Smith)
Porsche 911SC 'Super Carrera' – The Essential Companion (Streather)
Porsche 914 & 914-6: The Definitive History of the Road & Competition Cars (Long)
Porsche 924 (Long)
The Porsche 924 Carreras – evolution to excellence (Smith)
Porsche 928 (Long)
Porsche 930 to 935: The Turbo Porsches (Starkey)
Porsche 944 (Long)
Porsche 964, 993 & 996 Data Plate Code Breaker (Streather)
Porsche 993 'King Of Porsche' – The Essential Companion (Streather)
Porsche 996 'Supreme Porsche' – The Essential Companion (Streather)
Porsche 997 2004-2012 – Porsche Excellence (Streather)
Porsche Boxster – The 986 series 1996-2004 (Long)
Porsche Boxster & Cayman – The 987 series (2004-2013) (Long)
Porsche Racing Cars – 1953 to 1975 (Long)
Porsche Racing Cars – 1976 to 2005 (Long)
Porsche – The Rally Story (Meredith)
Porsche: Three Generations of Genius (Meredith)
Powered by Porsche (Smith)
Preston Tucker & Others (Linde)
RAC Rally Action! (Gardiner)
Racing Colours – Motor Racing Compositions 1908-2009 (Newman)
Rallye Sport Fords: The Inside Story (Moreton)
Roads with a View – England's greatest views and how to find them by road (Corfield)
Rolls-Royce Silver Shadow/Bentley T Series Corniche & Camargue – Revised & Enlarged Edition (Bobbitt)
Rolls-Royce Silver Spirit, Silver Spur & Bentley Mulsanne 2nd Edition (Bobbitt)
Rootes Cars of the 50s, 60s & 70s – Hillman, Humber, Singer, Sunbeam & Talbot (Rowe)
Rover P4 (Bobbitt)
Runways & Racers (O'Neil)
Russian Motor Vehicles – Soviet Limousines 1930-2003 (Kelly)
Russian Motor Vehicles – The Czarist Period 1784 to 1917 (Kelly)
RX-7 – Mazda's Rotary Engine Sportscar (Updated & Revised New Edition) (Long)
Singer Story: Cars, Commercial Vehicles, Bicycles & Motorcycle (Atkinson)
Sleeping Beauties USA – abandoned classic cars & trucks (Marek)
SM – Citroën's Maserati-engined Supercar (Long & Claverol)
Speedway – Auto racing's ghost tracks (Collins & Ireland)
Standard Motor Company, The Book of the (Robson)
Steve Hole's Kit Car Cornucopia – Cars, Companies, Stories, Facts & Figures: the UK's kit car scene since 1949 (Hole)
Subaru Impreza: The Road Car And WRC Story (Long)
Supercar, How to Build your own (Thompson)
Tales from the Toolbox (Oliver)
Tatra – The Legacy of Hans Ledwinka, Updated & Enlarged Collector's Edition of 1500 copies (Margolius & Henry)
Taxi! The Story of the 'London' Taxicab (Bobbitt)
This Day in Automotive History (Corey)
To Boldly Go – twenty six vehicle designs that dared to be different (Hull)
Toleman Story, The (Hilton)
Toyota Celica & Supra, The Book of Toyota's Sports Coupés (Long)
Toyota MR2 Coupés & Spyders (Long)
Triumph & Standard Cars 1945 to 1984 (Warrington)
Triumph TR6 (Kimberley)
Two Summers – The Mercedes-Benz W196R Racing Car (Ackerson)
TWR Story, The – Group A (Hughes & Scott)
Unraced (Collins)
Volkswagen Bus Book, The (Bobbitt)
Volkswagen Bus or Van to Camper, How to Convert (Porter)
Volkswagens of the World (Glen)
VW Beetle Cabriolet – The full story of the convertible Beetle (Bobbitt)
VW Beetle – The Car of the 20th Century (Copping)
VW Bus – 40 Years of Splitties, Bays & Wedges (Copping)
VW Bus Book, The (Bobbitt)
VW Golf: Five Generations of Fun (Copping & Cservenka)
VW – The Air-cooled Era (Copping)
VW T5 Camper Conversion Manual (Porter)
VW Campers (Copping)
Volkswagen Type 3, The book of the – Concept, Design, International Production Models & Development (Glen)
Volvo Estate, The (Hollebone)
You & Your Jaguar XK8/XKR – Buying, Enjoying, Maintaining, Modifying – New Edition (Thorley)
Which Oil? – Choosing the right oils & greases for your antique, vintage, veteran, classic or collector car (Michell)
Wolseley Cars 1948 to 1975 (Rowe)
Works Minis, The Last (Purves & Brenchley)
Works Rally Mechanic (Moylan)

www.veloce.co.uk

First published in 2017 by De Alk BV, Holland. This English language edition published in July 2018, reprinted October 2023 by Veloce Publishing Limited, Veloce House, Parkway Farm Business Park, Middle Farm Way, Poundbury, Dorchester, DT1 3AR, England. Tel +44 (0)1305 260068 / Fax 01305 250479 / e-mail info@veloce.co.uk / web www.veloce.co.uk or www.velocebooks.com.

ISBN: 978-1-787113-09-1 UPC: 6-36847-01309-7.

© 2018 & 2023 Arnoud op de Weegh, Ard op de Weegh and Veloce Publishing. All rights reserved. With the exception of quoting brief passages for the purpose of review, no part of this publication may be recorded, reproduced or transmitted by any means, including photocopying, without the written permission of Veloce Publishing Ltd. Throughout this book logos, model names and designations, etc, have been used for the purposes of identification, illustration and decoration. Such names are the property of the trademark holder as this is not an official publication. Readers with ideas for automotive books, or books on other transport or related hobby subjects, are invited to write to the editorial director of Veloce Publishing at the above address.

British Library Cataloguing in Publication Data – A catalogue record for this book is available from the British Library. Typesetting, design and page make-up all by Veloce Publishing Ltd on Apple Mac.
Printed and bound by CPI Group (UK) Ltd, Croydon, CR0 4YY.

ARNOUD OP DE WEEGH
& ARD OP DE WEEGH

Schlumpf

THE INTRIGUE BEHIND THE MOST BEAUTIFUL CAR COLLECTION IN THE WORLD

TABLE OF CONTENTS

Preface 6
The Schlumpf affair – two men in search of the truth 10
The years leading toward success, followed by
   inevitable decline 20
The game begins 26
The smear campaign against the Schlumpfs 34
Value of the collection 42
Sorting out a few things 46
Epilogue 54

Momentanément Volée 57

Birth of the collection 58
The largest purchase 63
The Malmerspach collection 68

Car descriptions 73

1937 Bugatti T57C Stelvio 74
1929 Lancia Dilambda 78
1936 Alfa Romeo 6C2300 B Lungo Pinin Farina 82
1936 Lancia Astura Pinin Farina 86
1937 Auto Union Wanderer W25K 90
1937 Bugatti T57 Ventoux 94
1937 Cord 812 Supercharged 98
1936 Maserati 4CM 102
1939 Mercedes-Benz W154 Silver Arrow 106
1929 Bugatti T35B 110
1933 Bugatti T41 Royale Park Ward 114
1953 Ferrari 250MM 118
1955 Gordini T32 F1 122
1936 Alfa Romeo 8C2900A Pinin Farina 126
1955 Mercedes-Benz 300 SL Gull Wing 130

About the authors 134
Acknowledgements 136

List of the collection 139

List of the Mulhouse museum collection 140
List of the Malmerspach collection 150
Cité de l'Automobile, collection Schlumpf 154

Index 159

Preface

Hans (left) and Fritz Schlumpf in the 1960s. (Photo collection Patenostre)

Much has been written about the Schlumpf collection and the way in which it came into being. There is agreement on one thing: the Schlumpf brothers did bring together a magnificent collection of automobiles – perhaps the most beautiful in the world. In this respect, all automobile enthusiasts owe a debt of gratitude to the Schlumpf brothers, especially to Fritz. Nevertheless, to this day the collection's reputation remains blemished, more or less artificially. A fraudulent bankruptcy allegedly made the collection possible, at the expense of workers. From 1976 until at least 1992, the French government and trade unions did everything in their power to depict Fritz and Hans Schlumpf as big capitalists who did not hesitate to put their pathological urge to collect before the interests of their workers. This approach has been successful because almost all publications continue to take the side of the French government, unions, and workers. And that is certainly the safest and easiest way to feel in the right: the angry capitalist versus helpless workers. It is the image that French socialism badly needed after the many years of Gaullism. During his election campaign François Mitterrand paid a visit to the museum that, at the time, was occupied by workers. But under the presidency of Christian-Democrat Valéry Giscard d'Estaing as well, harsh measures were taken, as of 1976, against the Schlumpfs. Was this done in answer to the increasingly influential role of socialism led by Mitterrand? After 1981 – when Mitterrand became president – all floodgates seemed to be opened. During a 1982 visit to the museum he lamented: "How could this happen?"

Actually, characterising the affair as an example of

Fritz Schlumpf in his Bugatti T35B during one of the many races in which he participated. (Photo collection Patenostre)

the 'rich capitalist versus the helpless workers' was a perfect fit: showing the Schlumpfs in a bad light, and the French government and trade unions as protectors of defenceless workers. But was it really about these workers, or were there other political or economic reasons?

Why was there no interest in the persons who wanted to buy the entire collection and pay its actual value? That money could have relaunched the factories and allowed the employees to keep their jobs. Why was the museum sold at a ridiculous price to the association that now manages it, leaving the workers – whose interests seemed at first to be the focus of attention – out in the cold? Did the Schlumpfs really not care about their employees? Did the brothers' desire to collect automobiles cause the Schlumpf empire's bankruptcy, or was it simply the crisis in the textile industry, which, in the mid-1970s, led to the demise of many European textile factories? Was the collection really funded by money from the workers, or did the factories' owners, who for years had also borne the financial risks, use their private money to acquire the automobiles? Did Fritz Schlumpf get a fair chance in the many court cases against him and should these cases have taken place at all? Why did the French judiciary not call on Swiss colleagues to try the brothers? What does the case look like when we reconsider it critically, almost 40 years later? This book attempts to answer all these questions, especially the most important one: Should there have been a Schlumpf affair?

During the more than nine years of our investigation we noticed that the case remains quite sensitive. After our written request in December 2011 to visit the museum's reserve collection in order to photograph it was initially approved, we received a telephone call shortly before our trip to Mulhouse to inform us that we would not be welcome after all. In other respects there was obstruction as well, and most Frenchmen who were willing to assist us, definitely did not want to be mentioned by name.

In our book we will try, 40 years after the events, to shed a different light on the entire affair, in which the Schlumpfs did not stand a chance. Fritz Schlumpf's most serious mistake was to believe that everything belonging to him actually was his. In France it was not seen that way.

Ard and Arnoud op de Weegh

Bugatti T35B Grand Prix (#4933, personal car of Fritz Schlumpf). (Photo collection Op de Weegh)

The Schlumpf affair – two men in search of the truth

After we published, together with Kay Hottendorff, our book on Michel Dovaz's mysterious collection (*The Fate of the Sleeping Beauties*), more and more people asked us to investigate the real course of events with regard to the Schlumpf collection and the Schlumpf affair. Initially, we were not enthusiastic. The story of the two brothers and their automobile collection had been milked dry, and judgement had been passed everywhere. Occasionally, an article, such as the one by Erwin Ulrix in the Dutch magazine *Het Automobiel* (vol 11, no 126), tentatively shed a different light on the matter, but most books and articles condemned the brothers' pathological collecting, and, at the time, we had no reason to doubt those views. Yet, several people in France, and a number of Bugatti owners, kept encouraging us to conduct a thorough investigation. In France it was in particular the surgeon André Dufilho, a friend of the Schlumpf family and passionate Bugattist, who put pressure on us. In the Netherlands it was the prominent Bugattist Kees Jansen, who, among other things, can claim credit for the Dutch Bugatti registers.

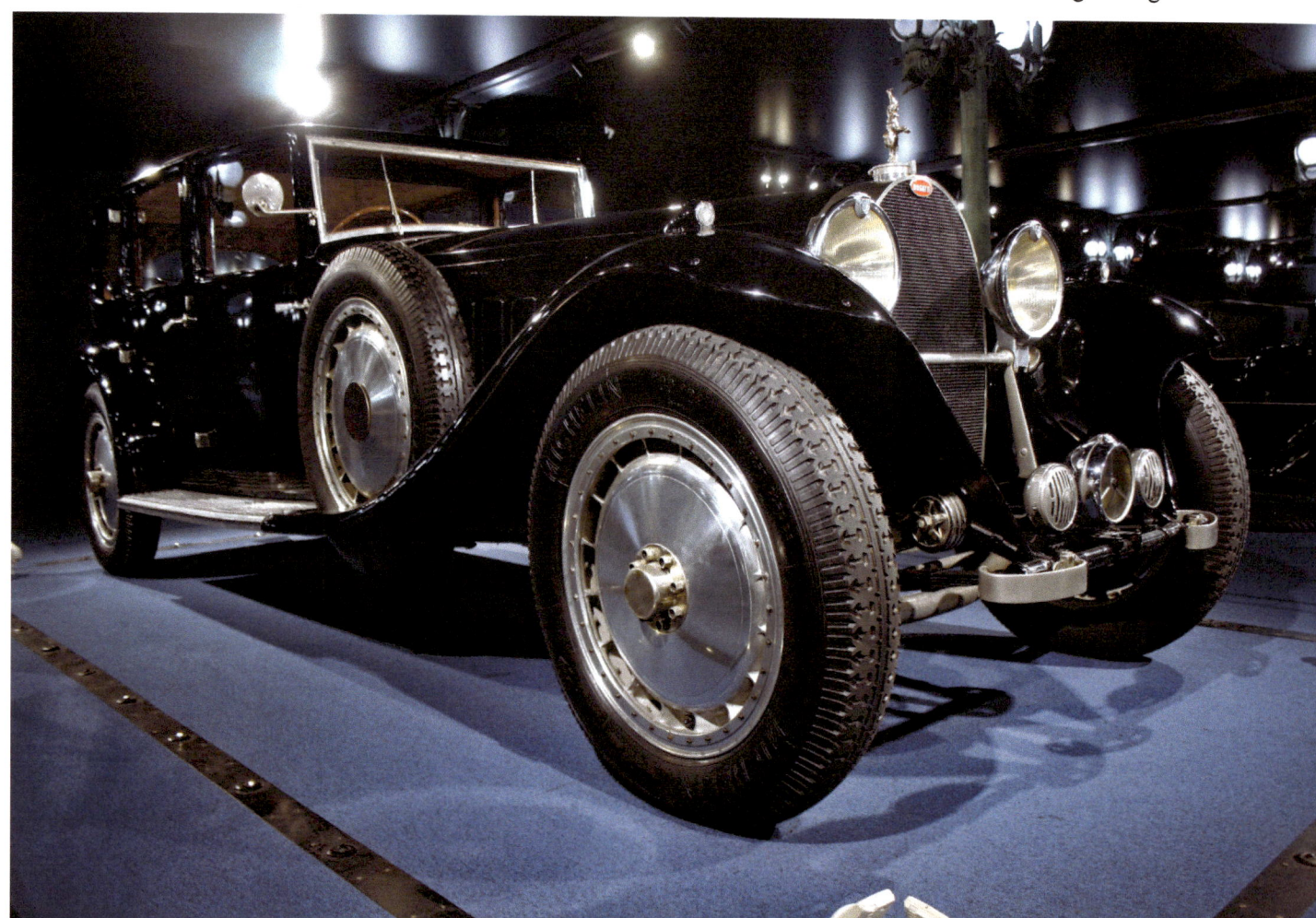

The automobile world's holy grail: Bugatti T41 Royale Park Ward. (Photo collection Op de Weegh)

Ard op de Weegh (left) visiting the Malmerspach collection in 2008; the other person is Jaap Braam Ruben.
(Photo collection Op de Weegh)

Eventually, in 2009, we decided to visit Mulhouse. We were greatly impressed by the enormous collection, which included a very large number of Bugattis. It made us look more closely again at the affair, and it did not take us much time to notice that the conclusions drawn in the past were very simplistic and one-sided. In exchange for our pictures of the Malmerspach collection, which Jaap Braam Ruben and Bruno Vendiesse had allowed us to take in August 2008, we received from Richard Adatto, who acted on behalf of Peter Mullin, an enormous amount of Schlumpf correspondence that covered several years. Several things became clear. Fritz Schlumpf had been able to buy several of his cars at a low price, and, after the workers' takeover, some parties outside France were interested in purchasing the entire collection at market value, or were willing to pay millions for the right to operate the museum for 25 years. This is in sharp contrast to the ridiculously low amount paid to transfer the collection in the 1980s to the association that runs the museum to this day. This money could have relaunched the factories and helped the workers – whose interests, supposedly, were most important. A simple export ban, however, torpedoed all foreign interest in the collection.

We also discovered that an Englishman – in the mid-1970s, when the Schlumpf factories were having serious difficulties – had been contacted and had agreed to buy part of the collection in order to keep the factories open. This buyer was even ready to purchase the entire collection and – believe it or not – Fritz Schlumpf was willing to agree. We will

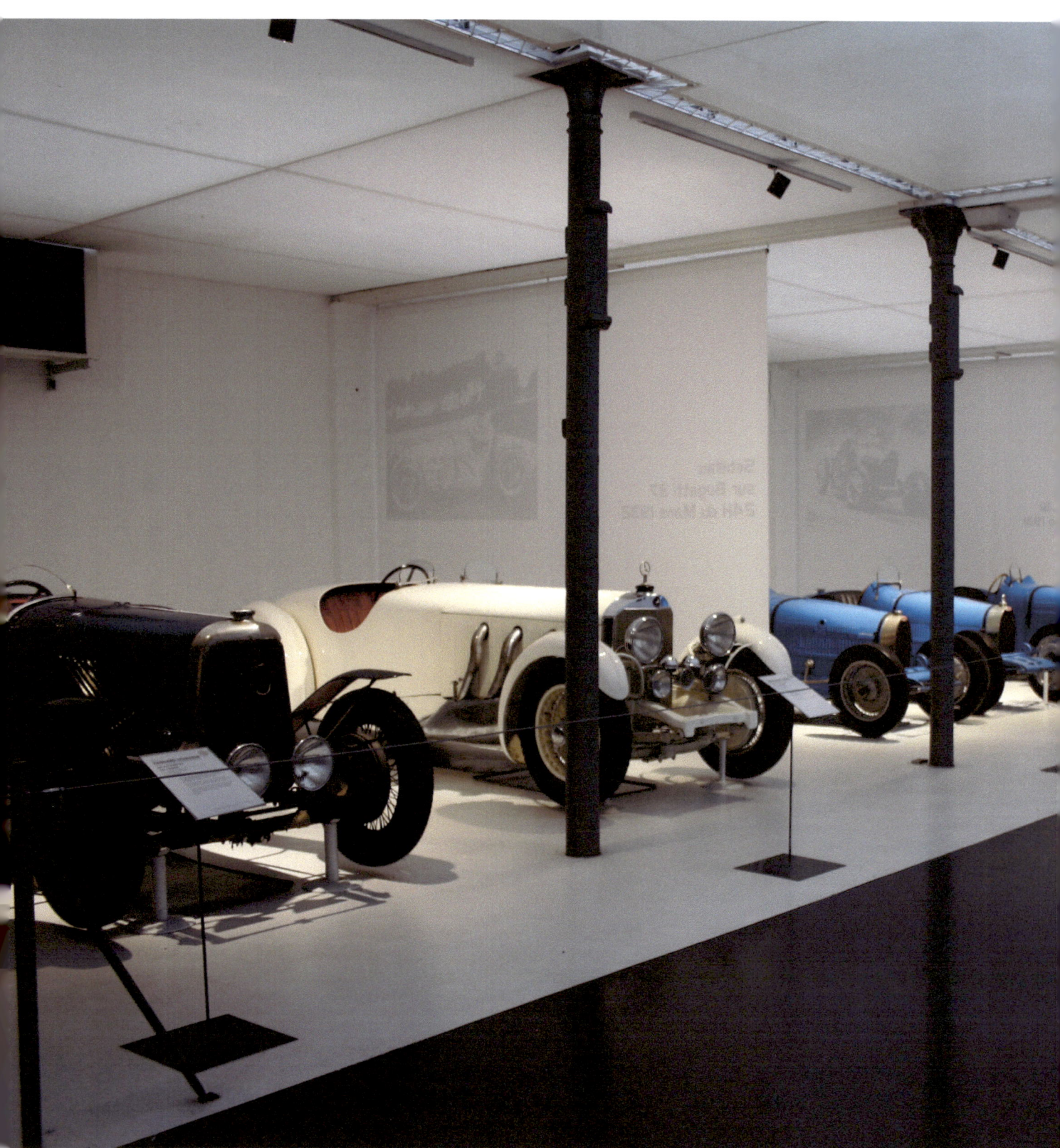

Some of the fabulous Grand Prix racers in the Schlumpf collection. (Photo collection Op de Weegh)

return to this topic later in the book. Knowing all this, we became increasingly convinced that events in the 1970s and '80s were very different to what history had made us believe.

At that point we did something that, in hindsight, we regretted. To start the discussion and to receive perhaps some more information we contacted Jacques Prost, a reporter for the *Journal d'Alsace*, a newspaper in the region where the affair had happened – in the lion's den, so to speak. On Sunday, March 28, 2010, this French journalist published in his paper what we had discovered so far. This included the fact that, in 1976, an Englishman had wanted to buy part of the collection, and that, with this sale, Fritz and Hans Schlumpf had wanted to save their factories, or at least be able to pay the workers three months' salary in case of a closure, which, at that time, was a rather generous gesture. Other textile factories that had gone bankrupt during those years did not even consider such a thing. The newspaper article was considered tantamount to heresy. In addition to compliments, we received all sorts of terrible curses. But, worse than that, places from where, until then, we had innocently requested and received information, now kept their doors closed to us. From that moment on, people in France knew that the two Dutchmen – who previously had unravelled the mystery surrounding Michel Dovaz's automobile collection – were now probing the Schlumpf affair. The judicial archive in Colmar was unwilling or unable to provide us with verdicts in the court cases against Schlumpf. All our requests remained unanswered, although, according to European law, all cases become public after 25 years, unless there are urgent reasons for secrecy.

When, in December 2011, we travelled for the second time to Mulhouse in order to photograph the collection for our book, we also asked the museum for permission to photograph the reserve collection, which, to a large extent, still needed to be restored. Two days before our departure we received a telephone call, informing us that the request had been turned down. We went to Mulhouse on the day we had scheduled, and we are almost certain that we were being closely watched throughout that day. That, at least, was our very strong impression. The next day we met in Strasbourg with Mr Martin Meyer (one of the Schlumpf family's attorneys), who, in a frank, one-hour conversation, told us about the affair. Among

A look at the museum's reserve collection in Mulhouse, which contains immensely valuable automobiles that have hardly been shown to the outside world. (Photo collection Heinz W Jordan)

Opposite: Present-day entrance to the Schlumpf museum in Mulhouse. (Photo collection Op de Weegh)

other things he mentioned that the sum received in 1999 by Arlette Schlumpf (Fritz's widow) from the French government was "the positive balance of the 1977 bankruptcy of the Schlumpf factories." He repeated this statement in a documentary about the affair in the autumn of 2015 on France 3. This sum, in 1999, amounted to 40 million French francs (on today's market between six and seven million euros). Is there anyone who knows of another bankruptcy involving such an enormous positive balance? It became obvious to us that there should never have been a bankruptcy, but only factory closings because they were no longer profitable. In short, the affair looked more and more fishy. Nevertheless, it remained a delicate business to write the book. That the affair was still very much alive after more than 35 years, and that there were many persons who did not want any investigation, was evident from the opposition and obstruction we encountered during the more than nine years of our investigation. But that motivated us to persevere all the more. The real break-through that provided conclusive evidence that the Schlumpfs should be seen very differently came in January 2017. For the second time we came into contact with Kevin Wheatcroft. He was present when, in 1976, his father Tom Wheatcroft first wanted to buy from Fritz Schlumpf a part of the collection and then all of it. More about this in a later chapter.

In coping with such hard to manage material it is good to work with another person. We both wanted to abandon the project, at different times and independent of each other, when encountering so much opposition to our investigations. There were many setbacks, and we realised that everything had

Luxury cars from the 1930s in the Schlumpf museum; note the gorgeous lamp posts that Fritz had fashioned after those of the Alexander III Bridge in Paris. (Photo collection Op de Weegh)

Fritz and Arlette Schlumpf, living in Switzerland after the 'affair.' (Photo collection Patenostre)

to be right. We also realised (this made things extra difficult) that the French government, the city of Mulhouse, and the trade unions would not be happy with our disclosures. Nevertheless, we did persevere, and now we are glad that we did not give up. We have rehabilitated Fritz, Hans, and their families, just as in 2008 we rehabilitated Michel Dovaz. That is what everyone deserves.

John W Shakespeare watching his Bugattis as they leave for France. (Photo collection David Gulick)

The years leading toward success, followed by inevitable decline

Hans and Fritz in their teens. (Photo collection Patenostre)

Hans Schlumpf was born in 1904, Fritz in 1906, in the Italian town of Omegna, near Milan. Their Swiss father, Carl Schlumpf, was a textile engineer, and their French mother, Jeanne Becker, was from Alsace. After their father's premature death, Jeanne returned to Mulhouse with her sons, where she earned a living as the owner of a flower shop. Hans initially worked in banking, while Fritz focused on the textile industry.

Later, both brothers conducted business all over Europe, and quickly became quite affluent. They invested their money in shares of textile factories, and bought companies that suited their business. In short, within 50 years they managed to control almost the entire woollen industry in northern France. Their success was due, in part, to their innate business instinct, but also due to their mother (a strong driving force in their lives until her death in 1957). Furthermore, their Swiss citizenship meant that they did not have to serve in the military in WWII, and could continue to strengthen their careers during the war years. Incidentally, due to the fact that they made flags for the Germans during the war years, they were, for a short time, considered collaborators, but were soon exonerated.

Europe's economy became stronger again after the war. The Schlumpf brothers' goods were once again in demand, and their wealth grew even faster. This did not mean, however, that they treated their workers badly. They paid them salaries that were at the time common in this branch of industry. They built homes for them, provided gifts at Christmas (also for the workers' children), organised excursions with all employees, and even purchased an ambulance to transport sick workers or their families to hospital. Fritz, though, was an old-fashioned boss, somewhat authoritarian, who did not want to be contradicted. That was not unusual in those years, though, and was perhaps not surprising given that he was the one who provided the capital for his companies, thus creating more than 2000 jobs, and bore all financial risks.

Hans (left) and Fritz with one of the workers' groups. (Photo collection Patenostre)

Fritz did not want to have anything to do with unions, and so his attitude towards his workers hardened from the mid-1960s on. His brother Hans was reputed to be somewhat softer, but he dealt primarily with the company's finances, whereas Fritz was in charge of the day-to-day running. That Fritz did not spend company money on automobiles was clear on June 21, 1971, when – with most of the collection already in their possession – the brothers were still financially able to acquire the crown jewel of the Alsatian textile industry – the Glück spinning mills – of which Fritz became the uncrowned 'Swiss King.' Needless to say, this caused much jealousy amongst the Mulhouse bourgeoisie, and, more specifically, amongst his competitors.

The crisis that was going to hit the textile industry all over Europe was not far away, though, and, in 1974 the first setbacks arrived in the form of much cheaper Asian textile goods. European textile companies fell in droves. The brothers' companies were facing hard times as well. So, in an ultimate attempt to pay the incurred business debts, Fritz Schlumpf and Tom Wheatcroft agreed, in 1976, on a loan with 33 cars as collateral. This would have enabled the Schlumpfs to pay the workers three months' salary, in the case of factory closings. The sale of the entire collection would have saved the factories. French officials refused, however, to issue an export permit, and the agreements came to nothing. In all likelihood these authorities must have understood at the time that their way of dealing with the situation would spell the end of the Schlumpf empire, with all its negative implications for the workers.

Because bankruptcy seemed inevitable – and because the banks in Mulhouse no longer wanted to help – Hans and Fritz resigned from their textile empire's board of directors in June 1976, and put the company up for sale for one French franc. So it was that, in the first half of 1976, what became known as the 'Schlumpf affair' began, with many people telling their own stories. It's too bad that the Schlumpfs, because of the circumstances and because of their character and pride, never told theirs. The lie had been born.

Fritz Schlumpf in his Bugatti T35B.
(Photo collection Patenostre)

Bugatti T35B. (Photo collection Op de Weegh)

1908 Panhard-Levassor race car. (Photo collection Op de Weegh)

1928 Bugatti T28.
(Photo collection
Op de Weegh)

1912 Bugatti T16.
(Photo collection
Op de Weegh)

The game begins

The Schlumpf brothers initially intended to close their factories in a fair manner, and to continue to pay the workers their salaries for three months. However, because the French authorities did not allow the deal between Tom Wheatcroft and Fritz Schlumpf, this did not happen. The export permit was bluntly refused. It is extra painful that, for the same reason, the sale of the entire collection to Wheatcroft did not take place either. Tom Wheatcroft passed away several years ago, but his son, Kevin, who was also present at the negotiations in 1976, wrote to us about these meetings:

"It is true my father was in deep negotiations with both Schlumpf brothers. Mr Schlumpf had written his bank details in a meeting with my father (at which I was present). The bank details were in order for my father to transfer funds to the Schlumpf account for the purchase of the entire collection. My memories are a little sketchy but initially my father, Tom, offered to loan money to the brothers in order that they could pay their debts. We were to take 33 cars out of the collection as a guarantee. As the evening progressed, Fritz Schlumpf announced that for a certain price he would now be prepared to sell us the entire collection. My father and Fritz shook hands on a deal and Fritz handed him his personal bank details in order that my father could transfer the funds. Fritz then entertained

Reminders of the large textile factories are still clearly visible in Malmerspach, even some 40 years after the affair. (Photo collection Op de Weegh)

us into the early hours of the morning, they seemed very relaxed that they had done a deal and Fritz bestowed many gifts on my father, photographs, car mascots, etc, etc. We immediately telephoned our bank to arrange transfer, subject to an agreement we were having drawn up with our lawyers. Within the space of three or four days Fritz contacted my father to say he was having difficulties releasing the collection and the deal would have to be postponed. We understood that the city of Mulhouse and the French government were the problem. Fritz said the government had told him nothing could be released. We immediately returned to the Schlumpfs for further negotiations, and it was quite clear from Fritz's demeanour that he felt betrayed and destroyed by the authorities. My father even returned the gifts to Fritz, but he would not accept them back. I particularly remember one of the female companions of Fritz, I'm unsure if she was his wife or girlfriend, she was so emotionally upset that they both had to leave the lunch until she could compose herself."

The woman to whom Kevin refers in the last lines was Fritz's wife Arlette, who was many years younger than he.

Without doubt, then, it was the city of Mulhouse and the French government that prevented the deal and wrote the overture to an opera from which they would later distance themselves. For the workers the curtain fell. The factories were closed and 2000 people were out of work – without any money, let alone the three months' salary that Fritz and Hans had wanted to pay. There were others who showed an interest in purchasing the collection, or part of it, but in those cases nothing happened either, for the same reasons.

Quite cleverly, Hans and Fritz were blamed for the affair. The trade unions were incited, even though the French government and the city of Mulhouse knew better, and, in turn, these unions incited the workers. That was not very difficult, of course, the brothers being regarded as capitalists who enriched themselves at the expense of the common man. All of this led to a very grim atmosphere. Persons who remained unknown even killed deer close to the Schlumpf home. On February 12, 1977, a young Swiss journalist writing for a Swiss paper entered, via an air shaft, the museum that Fritz had been building so carefully since approximately 1970. This Jorg Peter

Arlette Schlumpf – a dignified Française her entire life. (Photo collection Dufilho)

Arlette and Fritz Schlumpf during the period of the legal cases. (Photo collection Op de Weegh)

Lienhart could, for some 15 minutes, freely take all kinds of photographs. To this day he is proud of his break-in. Without any research he remains convinced that the automobiles had been purchased at the workers' expense. He ignores two essential points. The owner who provides capital and bears risks is also the owner of the company's assets and liabilities. Furthermore, most cars were purchased at a low price in comparison to their later value, and were restored in-house. The only things for which Fritz Schlumpf might be blamed is that he allegedly took some money from the pension fund – this was, of course, inexcusable, but he certainly wanted to redeposit the sum – and that he had some of his employees work, in the then empty factory in Mulhouse, on the restoration of cars and on the transformation of the building into a museum. He could have solved the first problem with the sale of one valuable car, but as was already pointed out, the French government and the city of Mulhouse did not permit this, and the second situation was something that happened in other companies as well. But the harm had been

The magnificent Bugatti T41 Royale Coupé Napoléon shortly after the workers' takeover in 1977.
(Photo collection Op de Weegh)

done. The day after the break-in the *Journal d'Alsace* published a short article and photographs, and Mr Lienhart received all the attention for which he had been clamouring for two years – that is how long he had been pursuing his smear campaign. It's true that the police briefly held him in custody, but that hardly bothered him. Apparently, Mulhouse in those days did not consider a break-in a very serious offence. Unions and workers contacted him and asked him to help them get access to the museum. Eventually they did this, in a different way, on March 7, 1977.

They forced entry through the gate onto the factory's premises, held three guards, then forced entry into the museum. We understand the emotions of the jobless workers when they saw the opulence. In their place we would probably have had the same feelings. That is human and entirely understandable. In that sense it is also understandable that the workers publicly set one of the cars on fire. Yet it remains strange that French authorities, the local police, and the city of Mulhouse did not intervene in this illegal occupation. Political motives?

Luxury from the 1930s in the museum in Mulhouse; note the different bodies. (Photo collection Op de Weegh)

Bugatti T41 Royale Park Ward just after the workers' takeover in 1977 – once an automobile for royalty; but in 1977 only one of the Schlumpfs' cars. (Photo collection Op de Weegh)

1953 Gordini type 26S.
(Photo collection Op de Weegh)

1953 Gordini type 23S.
(Photo collection Op de Weegh)

1953 Gordini type 24S.
(Photo collection Op de Weegh)

1955 Bugatti T251. (Photo collection Op de Weegh)

The smear campaign against the Schlumpfs

Shortly after the events detailed in the previous chapter, the workers besieged the Schlumpf family's villa in Malmerspach. The situation became very threatening. Hans and Fritz called the local police for help. They came after some time and actually did not know anything better to suggest than to advise the family to go to Switzerland, where they took up residence in the Drei Könige hotel in Basel. The police escorted the family to the Swiss border. Shortly thereafter, a warrant was issued in France to arrest Fritz and Hans, but because of their Swiss citizenship this did not yet have any implications for them. Their stay in Switzerland would last more than ten years. Hans passed away in 1989 and Fritz in 1992.

Meanwhile, the unions and workers had opened the museum to the public. Upon paying a small admission fee and listening to a biased story, visitors could look at the excesses of capitalism. François Mitterrand, too, visited the museum during his election campaign. How could he better demonstrate the way in which capitalists enriched themselves at the expense of workers. Articles and books were written, all carrying the same message: the fraudulent acquisition of this immense, beautiful car collection at the expense of workers. And that was said even though the Schlumpfs had demonstrated to have a greater concern for these people's interests than the government, the city of Mulhouse, or the unions, which had let themselves be manipulated for political reasons. The workers kept the museum open for two years. During that time the museum earned the equivalent of more than 396,331 pounds sterling for the CFTD (French trade union for textile workers).

Immediately thereafter – in March 1979 – David and Howard Cohen tried to buy the rights to operate the museum for a 25-year period. Not a bad idea, because the museum would stay in Mulhouse, in France, and there would be no problems regarding export permits (French patrimony). Nathaniel de Rothschild, of the bank in Paris that bears the same

Fritz Schlumpf's obituary (1992).

Fritz Schlumpf in the prime of life: 'Le Patron.'
(Photo collection Patenostre)

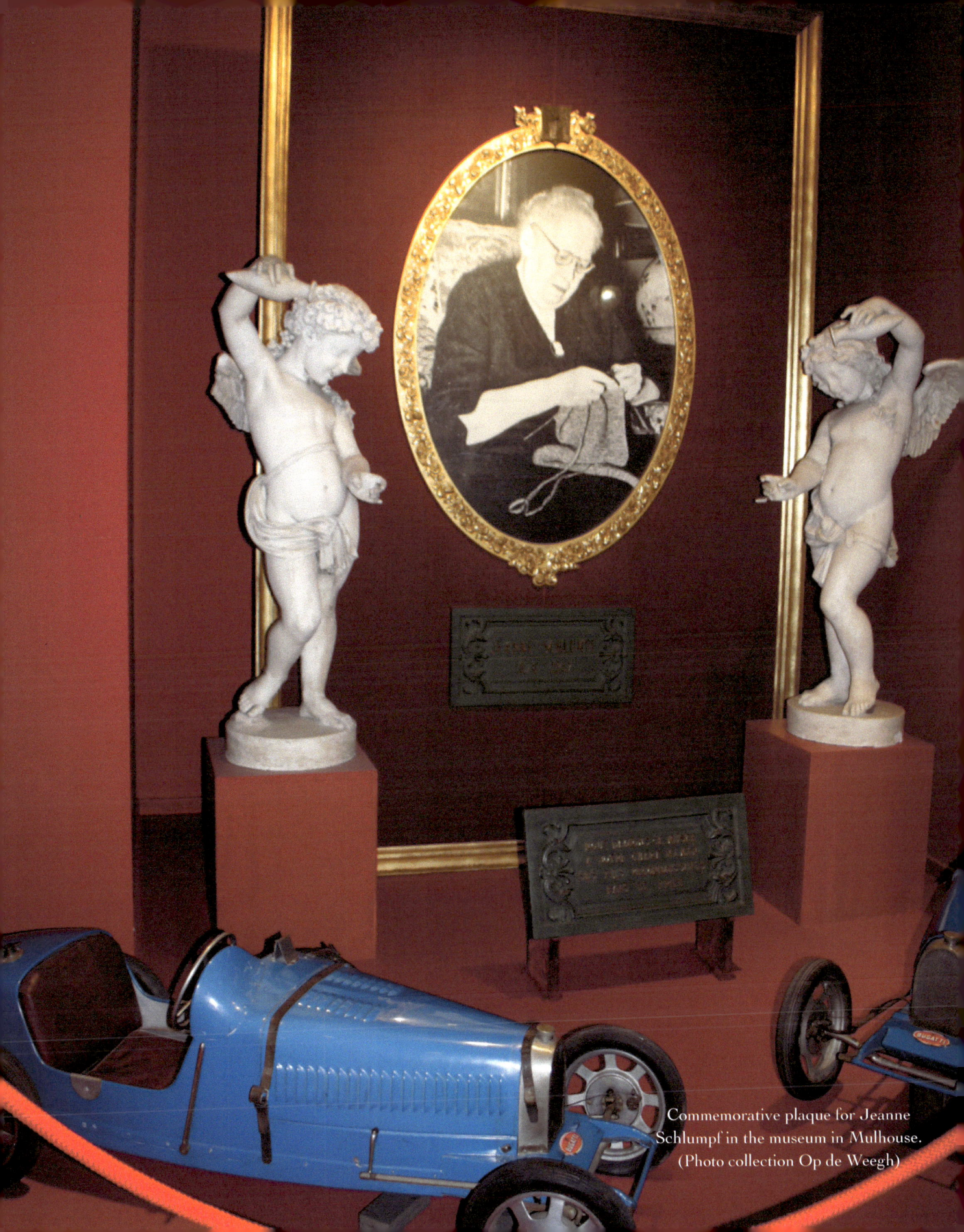

Commemorative plaque for Jeanne Schlumpf in the museum in Mulhouse. (Photo collection Op de Weegh)

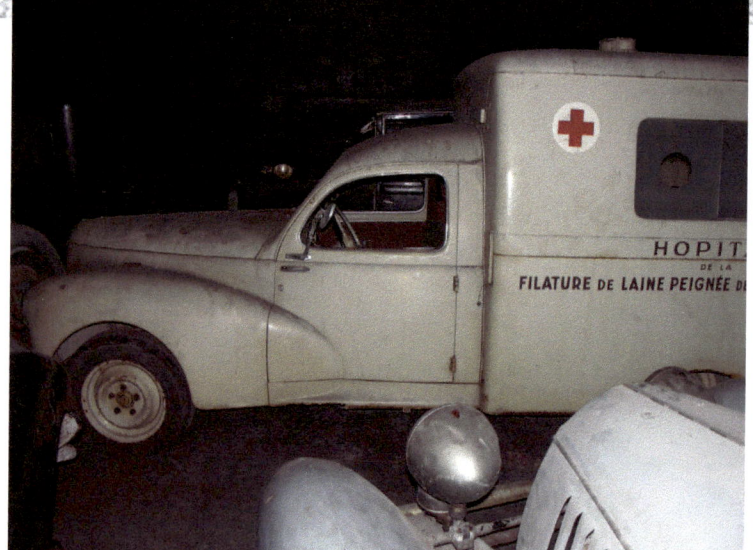

1911 Bugatti T19 bébé. (Photo collection Op de Weegh)

The Peugeot 203 ambulance that Hans and Fritz designated for their workers. (Photo collection Hottendorff)

name, personally offered to conduct the negotiations with the various parties on behalf of the Cohens. The sum under discussion amounted to a total of 20 million French francs – not a bad yield in those days.

The potential deal with the Cohens was not pursued, however. Strictly speaking, it might not have been possible anyway because, in an unusual way, the collection, apparently, was no longer the property of the Schlumpf brothers.

On April 8, 1981, a not-for-profit association

Fritz Schlumpf during his final visit (1990) to his collection in Mulhouse before his death, a very dignified man.
(Photo collection Peter Zinck)

comprising the French government, represented by the Ministère de la Culture et de la Communication, together with the Société Panhard, the Automobile Club de France, and the city of Mulhouse, bought the collection for 44 million French francs. However, to acquire it the right legal basis had to be found. And, when one keeps looking, one will eventually be successful. It is remarkable as well that Schlumpf actually won most legal cases, and a lot of questions may be asked about the court cases that he lost.

It looks as though some cases were initiated just to kick Schlumpf after he had gone down, or to keep the family name from being displayed on the museum's posters. Fritz did, however, win the court case about the latter issue, and, since that time, the collection has been known as: Musée National de l'Automobile/Collection Schlumpf.

In 1991, Fritz Schlumpf, already in very poor health, paid a surprise visit to the museum, on the occasion of the six Royales coming together. So, in spite of the numerous court cases, there was apparently no reason whatsoever to arrest the man (otherwise his enemies would undoubtedly have achieved this). To be on the safe side, though, Schlumpf was accompanied not only by his wife, Arlette, but also by his attorney, Martin Meyer, but nothing happened. This still remarkable man had the entire room under his spell when, in his wheelchair pushed by Arlette, he followed the itinerary he himself had designed, and stopped for several minutes in front of his mother's portrait. Everybody else was silent as well. That silence continued as he passed by the collection, and everyone could then hear his softly spoken words: "Momentanément volée" (temporarily stolen). And he was right. The only mistake he had made, was to think that what had once belonged to him really was his. He was allowed to think so as long as all the risks he took turned out well. But that changed when – through no fault of his own – he failed. At that moment, the legality of his possessions was questioned by people who made sure they would never take any risks themselves. The man did not even get the chance to use his personal belongings

One of the texts still in the museum in Mulhouse; very representative of the Schlumpf affair as it is still known today.
(Photo collection Op de Weegh)

in order to treat his workers fairly after the demise of his empire. That was made impossible by others, who put their political motives before the workers' interests, and also before the right to own property. These people claimed to protect the employees, but in reality wanted only to promote themselves. In this, they were successful for many years because, until today, there is still a strong belief that Fritz Schlumpf enriched himself at the expense of his workers, and then abandoned them to their fate without scruple.

Shortly thereafter Fritz passed away: a disillusioned man who never understood what he had done wrong. It's true that, because of his authoritarian and somewhat gruff manners, he did not always make friends. Furthermore, he only dealt directly with people he trusted and had personally selected, which outraged Mulhouse's bourgeoisie, as well as the bankers who, in 1976, cut off financial support. But this type of behaviour was normal for his generation of entrepeneurs.

After his death, his widow, Arlette, fought like a lioness to exonerate the Schlumpf name. She bought a house in Wettolsheim, in Alsace, where she would live until her death in 2008. In 1992, shortly after Fritz's passing, she achieved her first success. The name Schlumpf and the museum would forever be connected. In 1999 there was another success: the Malmerspach collection was returned to Arlette. This was the reserve collection of 63 vehicles that the French government confiscated in 1977. For some 22 years this collection was kept in poor storage conditions, with hardly any surveillance. Many parts of the automobiles were stolen, as was a special Alfa Romeo (which is described later in the book). Moreover, Arlette received the rather impressive sum of 40 million French francs. This was, according to one of the Schlumpf attorneys already quoted, "The positive balance of the 1977 bankruptcy." We would not mind going bankrupt in France! After 1999 Arlette became somewhat more conciliatory, as we see, for instance, in her posthumous book, *Auto biographie: pour l'amour de Fritz*.

Arlette and Fritz Schlumpf in the 1980s.
(Photo collection Dufilho)

Arlette in around 2006-2007.
(Photo collection Dufilho)

A row of Bugatti T35 automobiles in the Schlumpf museum, 1977.
(Photo collection Op de Weegh)

Value of the collection

When, on March 7, 1977, the workers forced entry into Fritz Schlumpf's well-guarded sanctuary, they must have been absolutely stunned, seeing such a magnificent collection of restored automobiles in almost perfect surroundings. The workers must have felt deeply hurt, first having lost their jobs, then seeing their boss' wealth. They had no idea that Fritz had been willing in 1976 to sell part of the magnificent collection to Tom Wheatcroft in order to pay them at least three months' salary, and had even reached an agreement with Wheatcroft to dispose of the entire collection. As was pointed out earlier in this book, these deals failed because of the French government's attitude. The workers could not know that it was precisely for that reason that their fate had been sealed. They only saw this opulence, which understandably outraged them. The unions, which were also deliberately kept in the dark, and thus could serve a higher political motive, only fanned the flames of hostility.

But what actually was the value of this immense collection? At what price had it been purchased and then restored? And how had the wonderful museum been built? Above all, how had all of this been

financed? Let us start by saying that Fritz and Hans Schlumpf were shrewd businessmen who amassed a huge fortune in the post-war years until the early 1970s, when the European textile industry started having great difficulties. This wealth had allowed them to purchase their automobiles, about which we should add that in the 1950s and '60s there was hardly any interest in old cars, so that they often could be acquired at very low prices. We now know that their value would greatly increase in the following decades, a trend that continues to this day. Fritz usually had his automobiles restored (if necessary) in-house, so that these costs were low as well.

A Mercedes-Benz 770K chassis (1978) in the Mulhouse museum's reserve collection; today, a car for the very rich collector.
(Photo collection Jean Marc Kohler)

Opposite: Bugatti T46 Coupé Superprofile in 1977. (Photo collection Op de Weegh)

In the late 1970s and early '80s, various experts appraised the collection. Twice this was done at the request of the French government, and twice at Fritz Schlumpf's request. The differences were gigantic. The appraisals for the government were alarmingly lower than those done on Schlumpf's behalf.

In March 1977 Poulain-Loudner, working for the French government, estimated the total value of the collection to be 56,786,900 French francs.

In July 1979 Chappelon, also working on behalf of the French government, arrived at a value of 39,697,000 French francs.

In December 1980 Fritz Schlumpf asked the undisputed expert Christian Huet to conduct an appraisal. He valued the collection at 305,915,600 French francs.

Another appraisal, again at Fritz Schlumpf's request, was done by Christie's – not exactly inexperienced – and the result was an estimate of 325,870,000 French francs.

For inexplicable reasons the appraisals done for the French government and those for Fritz Schlumpf are vastly different. Is this an example of 'who pays the piper calls the tune'? Were some appraisals manipulated? Fritz Schlumpf knew Christian Huet, but we cannot imagine that the latter would have risked tampering with an appraisal. He already had an excellent reputation, and, to this day, is considered an impeccable expert. Schlumpf's next move, when

A Bugatti T251 in the Mulhouse museum's reserve collection. (Photo collection Jean Marc Kohler)

he turned to Christie's, was a masterstroke. We think that nobody will have any doubts about the integrity of this auction house. We think, therefore, that the value of the collection around 1980 must have been at least 300,000,000 French francs. We will not comment here on the other appraisals and their origins and will leave it to the reader to draw their own conclusions. It remains curious, though, that, on April 8, 1981, the entire collection was sold to the Association pour le Musée National de l'Automobile de Mulhouse for 44 million French francs, which was close to the appraisals conducted for the French government and just slightly more than 12 per cent of the real value. In this not-for-profit association the French government has the authority to make decisions.

We have not been able to find out what was done with the money. It is doubtful that it went to the workers who had lost their jobs. Otherwise that would have been given a lot of attention and we would still know about it today.

Remarkable, too, is the fact that several automobiles listed in the 1977 and 1979 appraisals conducted for the French government were no longer there when Fritz Schlumpf had the collection appraised by Huet and Christie's. Where did these cars go? Had they been sold, and, if so, by whom? Was the sale of these automobiles allowed? Where did the money go? Even after the museum was sold to the association, in 1981, several vehicles were sold, although this should not have happened. The collection, including the reserve collection, was supposed to have remained intact. Because we do not want to cause problems for the present owners, we will not mention any automobiles or names. But it is strange.

The Bugatti T251's impressive front. (Photo collection Jean Marc Kohler)

Sorting out a few things

Fritz and Hans Schlumpf intended to pay workers their salaries for three months after factory closures. To that end, they wanted to get a loan from Tom Wheatcroft, with 33 of their automobiles as collateral. The French government refused to approve an export permit, and rumour had it that the vehicles had already been mortgaged. But if that had been the case, the creditors would certainly have presented a claim at the time of the sale to the not-for-profit association formed by the city of Mulhouse, the Société Panhard, the Automobile Club de France, and the French government. Needless to say, ultimate authority regarding the collection is in the hands of the French government.

In 1976 Fritz wanted to sell the entire collection to Tom Wheatcroft. The refusal of an export permit made this impossible.

The factories should not have been declared bankrupt. In 1999 there turned out to be a positive balance of 40 million French francs, which Arlette received, together with the Malmerspach collection.

There were four appraisals between 1977 and 1981. We have all four – two were conducted at Fritz Schlumpf's request, by well-known experts, while the other two were done on behalf of the French government. The former two (including the one by Christie's) were eight times higher than those conducted for the French government. Yet, the collection was then sold to the association that still owns it for a sum that corresponded to the low appraisals. Fritz did try, with the help of a bank guarantee, to buy the collection at the same price.

No automobiles in the collection were supposed to be sold. We discovered, however, that several in the museum, as well as some in the reserve collection, were.

Around the time of the confiscation, a South-African consortium led by David Cohen attempted to purchase the rights to operate the museum for a 25-year period, for the sum of 20 million French francs. The unions and workers were not told about this.

A selection of Gordini race cars in the Schlumpf collection. (Photo collection Op de Weegh)

In all the court cases against Fritz, he was found guilty only of having taken a small sum out of the pension fund – which he intended to redeposit – and of the fact that he had some 40 factory employees work every day on restorations. From a total of 2000 employees, this number is negligible. He could have solved the financial problems related to these cases by selling, for instance, a Bugatti T41 Royale.

When, in 1991, Fritz Schlumpf paid a visit to the museum, he did not encounter any difficulties. If he had really been found guilty of anything serious, he would certainly have been arrested.

In 1999, the Malmerspach collection was returned to Arlette Schlumpf, and she also received more than 40 million French francs. Would this have been done if Hans and Fritz Schlumpf had been proven guilty, and if they really had treated their workers as badly as had been alleged?

PRIVATE & CONFIDENTIAL

21, rue Laffitte, Paris 9e

March 30, 1979

Mr. Howard J. Cohen
2346 Mar East
Tiburon - California 94920

Mr. David Cohen
Dashing Centre
240 - Commissionner St.
Johannesburg

Dear Sirs:

Pursuant to our conversation, I am sending you a letter laying down the conditions under which Banque Rothschild would be happy to cooperate with you, and to help you in the acquisition of the Schlumpf Museum, which actually consists of :

. the Schlumpf car collection
. the building
. the land.

We shall readily assist you in any way you require and use our best efforts to implement this acquisition.

Our services will cover the following undertakings :

- approach individually each entity involved in this transaction (Syndic, Ministère de la Culture et de la Communication, Automobile Club de France, Ville de Mulhouse, etc...).

- supervise and coordinate with you the activities of the lawyers.

- structure the deal, setting up the necessary agreements, obtaining the Government approvals when required and arranging the most favorable financial plan.

.../

Société Anonyme au Capital de 63.125.000 F - R.C. Paris B 57.2054286 - L.B.F.N.396

Letter from Nathaniel de Rothschild, of the Banque Rothschild, confirming that his bank will assist in handling the various aspects of the brothers Cohen's offer to acquire the collection in Mulhouse for a 25-year period. (Op de Weegh archives)

21, rue Laffitte, Paris 9ᵉ

March 30, 1979 - 2

- advise and assist in matters pertaining to financial requirements, and when requested, aid in obtaining appropriate financing with regards to favorable terms and conditions.

In consideration of our services, you agree to pay Banque Rothschild a success fee, contingent upon the successful closing of this transaction.

This contingent success fee of 2,500,000 French Francs will be payable as follows :

1.- At least 40% at closing

2.- The remainder over a maximum five year indexed on the cost of living index (INSEE, Indice coût de la vie).

This fee is subject to a specific tax (V.A.T.) that will be collected at its current rate at the time of closing (the present rate is 17.60%).

If Banque Rothschild has to help you find additional investors, it shall be remunerated a specific placement fee of 5% of the amounts collected.

This agreement is valid for a period of six months from the date of signature, and is automatically renewed on a six month basis unless you advise us otherwise.

This agreement shall be governed and construed under the laws of France.

We hope this proposal will meet your approval and if you are in agreement with the text of this letter, please express your approval by signing and returning to us the copy of this letter keeping the original for your records.

Yours sincerely,

Nathaniel de ROTHSCHILD.

Agreed:

Mr. Howard J. Cohen

Mr. David Cohen

Christie's appraisal. (Op de Weegh archives)

```
                                    325,866.
            chassis sans référence         4.
                                    325,870.




ESTIMATION


TROIS CENT VINGT CINQ MILLIONS HUIT CENT        325,870,000F
SOIXANTE DIX MILLE FRANCS.

                        Christie, Manson and Woods ltd




8, King Street,
    St. James's,
        London, SW1Y 6QT.    - 31 -         JAN
```

```
Véhicules et pièces divers.
17 moteurs autre que Bugatti.
            Autro Daimler - Benz 1 cyl. - Benz 4 cyl. - Cord V8 -
            Daimler - Farman A6 B - Ferrari V 12 1500cc - Hispano-
            Suiza 12 Cyl. - Horch 12 cyl. - Lorraine 450 cv -
            Mathis 8640 - Maybach 12 cyl - Maybach 12 cyl - Maybach
            6 cyl. - Mercédès ! - Peugeot à bruleur - Serpollet -
            Talbot avion - Alfa Roméo - Mercédès course Simplex -
            Delaunay Belleville - de Dion Bouton - de Dion -
Pièces divers.
            Deux chars Sicilien - Deux pompe à "incendie"- Onze cycles
            du début du siècle ou de la fin du 19 en siècle - Six
            véhicules hippomobiles - divers éléments de carrosserie -
            Radiateur et pièces de Mercédès 770 - pièces Talbot -
            300 phares et lanternes ( environ ) - Radiateur de
            Farman - Pièces Renault - Pièces hippomobiles -
            Pièces divers de mécanique.

            Soit un montant représentant une somme d'environ:
                                4.000.000-Fr F
                    Report      301.915.000-Fr F
                    Total général 305.915.000-Fr F


            L'estimation ci-dessus, concerne entre autre, 539 véhicules
            automobile , dont 153 BUGATTI.

                    Additif page 28
```

Christian Huet's appraisal. (Op de Weegh archives)

Poulain-Loudner's appraisal.
(Op de Weegh archives)

V - RESULTATS -

La collection de voitures, chassis, moteurs et matériels divers que nous avons examinée dans les locaux du Musée SCHLUMPF à MULHOUSE a été évaluée à une somme totale de :

— 39.697.500 Fr.

qui se décompose ainsi :

- Musée   : 36.771.500 Fr.
- Ateliers : 2.926.000 Fr.

Les matériels construits par "BUGATTI" représentent une part importante de cette Collection.

  136 véhicules ou chassis complets pour : 20.566.000.—
   25 moteurs   —   —   pour :   545.500.—
   10 matériels ou groupes de matériels
       divers dont les 2 jouets pour :   119.000.—

  171 pièces   pour : 21.222.500.—

Pour les autres Marques nous avons trouvé :

  314 véhicules ou chassis complets pour : 17.821.500.—
    6 moteurs   —   —   pour :   88.000.—
   26 matériels ou groupes de matériels
       divers dont les motocyles, cycles   565.500.—
       et charettes.

  346 pièces   pour : 18.475.000.—

Total de l'ensemble de tous les véhicules et lots compris dans la collection :

   678 lots   pour   56 786 900 F.

Répartition qualitative   Répartition qualitative
       BUGATTI   NON BUGATTI

1. 135 lots : 21 355 500 F.   1. 259 lots : 24 684 100 F.
2. 14 lots : 1 213 000 F.   2. 61 lots : 1 800 500 F.
3. 66 lots : 4 843 000 F.   3. 143 lots : 2 890 800 F.

   215 lots   27 411 500 F.   463 lots   29 375 400 F.

   REPARTITION QUALITATIVE DE L'ENSEMBLE DE LA COLLECTION

       1. 394 .... 46 039 600 F.
       2.   75 ....   3 013 500 F.
       3. 209 ....   7 733 800 F.

            678   56 786 900 F.

Remarque :
Si nous conseillons de garder éventuellement les 4/7 environ de lots, cette proportion se chiffre à plus des 4/5 du montant total.

Chappelon's appraisal. (Op de Weegh archives)

1931 OM type 665 MM roadster. (Photo collection Op de Weegh)

1926 Panhard et Levassor monoplace 35 CV. (Photo collection Op de Weegh)

1937 Tatra T87. (Photo collection Op de Weegh)

1933 Mercedes-Benz 380 Cabriolet. (Photo collection Op de Weegh)

Epilogue

There are few collectors about whom more has been written than the Schlumpf brothers (particularly Fritz, the main scapegoat). We, too, initially believed the negative stories about the collection and the bankruptcy, because they all seemed to be confirmed by different sources. Our investigation took nine years, with fairly lengthy interruptions. We encountered a lot of opposition, and people who did want to provide information insisted on remaining anonymous. The Schlumpf family and attorneys also were reluctant to cooperate. After all, they had been subjected to all kinds of attacks for decades, and feared that another book would again cast aspersions on them. We fully understand their attitude. Fritz Schlumpf's son-in-law and granddaughter did not know us, and assumed that our enquiries could very well be another attack on the family, and that we, too, would perhaps once more spread the same lies. Under such circumstances it is very challenging for authors to remain motivated when they encounter such massive opposition and lack of cooperation.

Fortunately, though, there were two of us, so that we could, time and again, encourage each other to continue in order to reveal the hidden truth. We do not make a final judgement, but prefer to leave that to you. We do have the impression, however, that Hans and Fritz Schlumpf, their families, and their descendants have been, and continue to be, greatly wronged. We hope that Fritz and Arlette Schlumpf's granddaughter, Cléophée Hermann Schlumpf, will finally have peace and justice. We also hope that, on the basis of the information we provide in our book, those involved at the time will seriously reconsider which parties were the real culprits.

Whilst it's true that, since the early 1990s, the museum's name has included 'Schlumpf,' and, in 1999, Arlette Schlumpf received a rather large sum of money (the positive balance of the bankruptcy in the 1970s), as well as the Malmerspach collection, that did not mean that the full debt to the family had been paid off. The collection remains, inalienably, associated with one passionate automobile enthusiast: Fritz Schlumpf. He remains a presence in the museum, as its proud owner – at least, in our eyes. As he whispered during his final visit, this collection has only been 'momentanément volée' (temporarily stolen). He was very weak, sitting in a wheelchair, when he spoke these words, but because the people around him – who felt that this was the farewell visit by the real owner – remained completely silent, Fritz's words sounded like a loud indictment. The owner is dead. His courageous wife, Arlette, was eventually paid a sum that represents only a small portion of this immense collection's value. And Fritz and Arlette's granddaughter still has to live with the blemish that, for political reasons, continues to be associated with the name 'Schlumpf.'

We hope that this book will contribute to a balanced consideration of the 'Schlumpf affair.' And we are hopeful that the magnificent collection can cast off of the connotation of feudalism. Instead, it must become an homage to the man who brought it all together, and who will always be the moral owner of what, in all likelihood, is the most beautiful collection of cars in the entire world.

Opposite: 1899 Panhard et Levassor A2.
(Photo collection Op de Weegh)

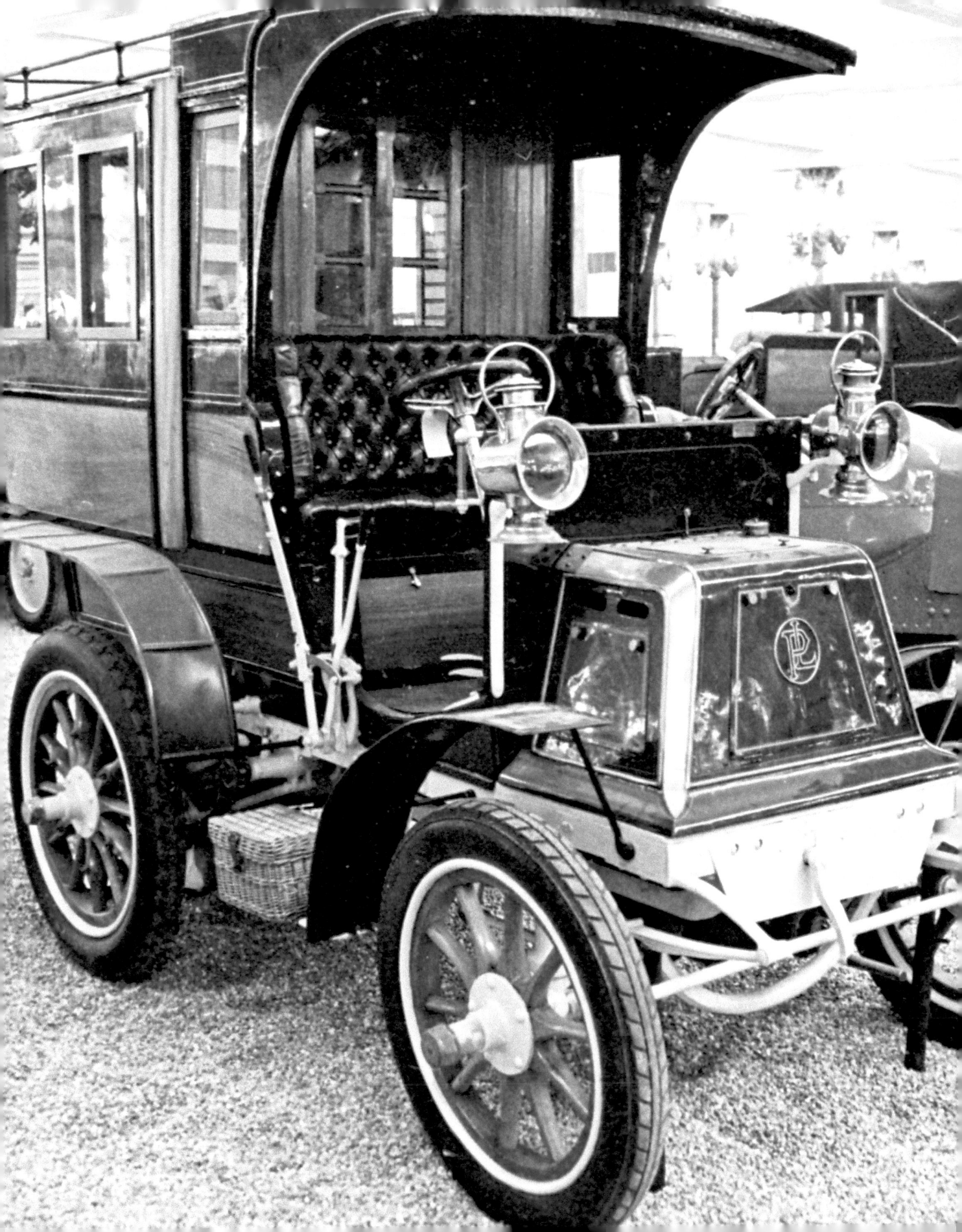

1904 Dufaux type 100/120.
(Photo collection Op de Weegh)

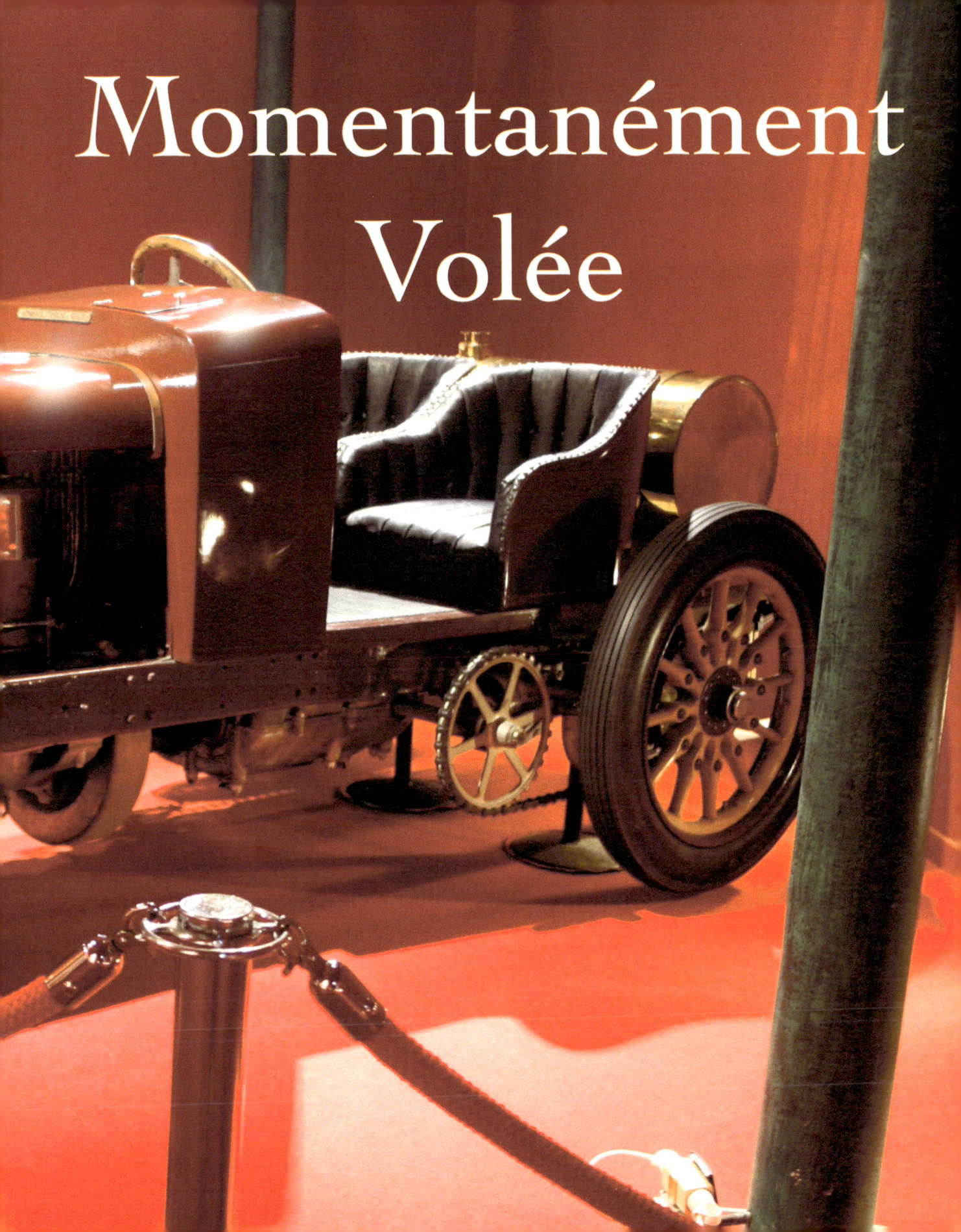

Momentanément Volée

Birth of the collection

Fritz had always been very interested in anything related to technology. Even before WWII he owned a Bugatti T35B, with license plate number 3842-PB5. This racing car is now in the museum.

After his mother's death in 1957, Fritz began to collect a few automobiles. According to some, he did this as compensation for the loss of his mother. Others claimed that Jeanne had always kept her sons under tight control because she was extremely frugal and expected that of them as well. Until about 1960 only a few automobiles were purchased, but that changed quickly. The brothers' urge to collect became pathological.

In the summer of 1960 Fritz met Mr Raffaelli. The latter was just selling a Renault Dauphine to a customer when a Mercedes 300 showed up. The reason was that in addition to running a Renault garage, Raffaelli owned a few Bugattis. Upon entering the garage, Schlumpf introduced himself: "My name is Fritz Schlumpf." Raffaelli answered: "Very nice to meet you, but please wait a moment

The magnificent Mercedes-Benz 300 SLR (W196S) that Fritz Schlumpf bought directly from Daimler in 1966. (Photo collection Op de Weegh)

A 1924 Renault Type 40 next to a 1920 Panhard Levassor X26. (Photo collection Op de Weegh)

because I am working with a customer ..." "You probably did not hear me. I am Fritz Schlumpf. I own factories. Hundreds of people work for me and listen to me whenever I talk to them." Raffaelli: "You should not expect that here because I am waiting on another customer. Please be patient." Although clearly annoyed, Schlumpf decided to wait because he understood that in southern France this man, Raffaelli, would be indispensable to him in his efforts to locate and purchase special old cars. Both men did learn to appreciate and respect each other, and Raffaelli later stated that he had been paid quite well by Schlumpf.

During that same summer of 1960 they agreed that Raffaelli and a friend of his would look out for automobiles that Schlumpf was interested in. In just a few months this resulted in a rather nice collection, including three Rolls-Royces, two Hispano-Suizas, one Tatra, and two Bugatti T57s. Eventually, there were 40 vehicles, including ten Bugattis, all ready to be driven. Besides Raffaelli, Schlumpf instructed other people to scout for cars. When interesting models were located, Fritz usually came to inspect them in person (often appearing arrogant and insensitive, which is evident in his correspondence with potential sellers).

At the time, there was little interest even in special old cars, so the investment he had to make was not enormous, which means that the collection's value in the 1970s was many times larger than the sums Schlumpf had paid. The best proof in this respect is the acquisition of the Shakespeare collection, about which we will say more later in the book. John Shakespeare wanted to sell his entire collection of 30 Bugattis for $105,000, whereas Fritz made an initial offer of $70,000. Because there were not many other offers, Schlumpf and Shakespeare started negotiating. They settled for $85,000, including shipping costs, which amounted to an average price of less than $3000 per automobile.

A year earlier, Fritz had seized another excellent opportunity. Ettore Bugatti, 'le Patron,' had died in 1947, and his company was not faring as well as it had before WWII. A lot of things had been tried, without much success. Hispano-Suiza bought the entire Bugatti company in 1962. A few years later Hispano-Suiza needed more space and, with the approval of Ettore Bugatti's heirs, sold everything, including the

Continued on page 62.

German pride: 1938 Mercedes-Benz 540K Cabriolet bodied by Erdmann et Rossi. (Photo collection Op de Weegh)

prototypes and all the family's personal automobiles. Because he made the highest bid (120,000 French francs), Schlumpf was able to obtain a lot that consisted of 18 Bugattis, amongst which was one of the six 'Royales.'

In 1987, a Bugatti type 41 Royale was auctioned at Christie's in London for 5.5 million pounds – proving again that the shrewd businessman Fritz Schlumpf had paid a pittance for the automobiles, in comparison to their value around 1980. The opulence that infuriated the workers on March 7, 1977, had been acquired for a fraction of its later value, and with the Schlumpfs' personal funds. The French government was aware of this, of course, and the city of Mulhouse probably knew this as well. However, it did not suit local and national strategy to share this knowledge with the unions and the workers, or to divulge that several parties were interested in buying the entire collection. Export permits were refused, and the Cohens, who wanted to manage the museum for 25 years on French soil, did not get anywhere either. Thus, it is doubly painful that two appraisals arrived at only one-eighth of the real value determined at a later time by Christian Huet and Christie's, the premier British auction house.

Here is the split: first, make the entire nation, the unions, and the workers believe that it is an enormous collection with an incredible value, which can only have been acquired at the expense of these same workers; next, conduct two appraisals that justify the sale of the entire collection to an association for only 40 million French francs – a sum that corresponds to the results of two appraisals. Here one must ask whether Huet and Christie's were completely wrong. We do not think so. Amazing is also the fact that the amount corresponds closely to the money Arlette Schlumpf received in 1999, which was described as the positive balance of the so-called bankruptcy. Bizarre and remarkable. And, by the way, we have not been able to find out what happened to the money that the association paid in 1981 to obtain the collection.

In 1961, the total collection consisted of 400 vehicles, and in 1966 there were 500. In 1967, the number of Bugattis alone amounted to 105. Thus, one may conclude without any doubt that the collection was established during the inexpensive years, and that after 1967 only a few more automobiles were purchased.

Fritz then started the creation of his magnificent museum, which in itself was an enormous operation. The collection is displayed in a hall that measures 17,000 square metres (182,986 square feet) and is lit by 900 bronze lamp posts, resembling those of the Alexander III Bridge in Paris. Every detail was taken into account, catering included. At the time of Jorg Peter Lienhart's break-in and the subsequent illegal occupation by the workers, 102 makes were represented, 66 of which were French. There were 112 Bugattis, 31 Daimler Benz, 26 De Dion Boutons, 14 Gordinis, 10 Ferraris, 8 Alfa Romeos, 8 Maseratis, amongst other marques.

The largest purchase

In the late 1950s and throughout the 1960s Fritz Schlumpf had people looking for special automobiles all over the world. When they found something interesting, they informed 'le Patron,' who was not always very diplomatic and friendly in the ensuing correspondence. Among other things, Fritz wanted to own many Bugattis. In 1964 an extraordinary opportunity presented itself. In the United States, John Shakespeare owned a collection of 30 Bugattis. In order to devote himself exclusively to his new hobbies, skiing and skydiving, he wanted to sell the cars. With Bob Shaw and Hugh Conway serving as intermediaries, difficult negotiations were conducted. Eventually there was a deal and on March 1, 1964, money and cars were exchanged. A sum of $85,000 was paid, which included shipping. For sentimental reasons John had tried to keep one car, a Bugatti 55, but Fritz was unrelenting.

If Shakespeare had known Schlumpf better, he would have understood that Fritz ultimately would have settled for 29 Bugattis. Yet Fritz was always such a tough negotiator that nobody imagined that his merciless attitude masked a man with a big heart for cars, in particular for Bugattis. In the December 1964 issue of *Sports Car Graphic*, the photographer who took a series of pictures when the 30 vehicles were put on a train, commented: "It was quite a spectacle, and a rather sad one for the 'aficionado,' because these cars, that once astounded the racing world, were leaving this country – probably for

Part of the Malmerspach collection, currently in the Mullin Museum in Oxnard.
(Photo collection Mullin Museum USA)

good." Regarding the last comment, David M Gulick turned out to be wrong because 44 years later several of these automobiles returned to the United States, when Bruno Vendiesse and Jaap Braam Ruben bought the Malmerspach collection (one of Schlumpf's reserve collections) from Arlette Schlumpf, then sold some of the vehicles to Peter Mullin, who has a wonderful museum in Oxnard, California.

On May 8, 1975, John Shakespeare, 69 years old, was found dead in his home, handcuffed and his ankles tied by an electrical cable. The cause of death

Beautiful display of unrestored 'Malmerspach automobiles' in the Mullin museum. (Photo collection Mullin Museum USA)

was a single 22-calibre bullet. Robbery was not the motive because nothing was taken from his home.

A few people thought that the case, which to this day has not been solved, might be related to the 1964 transaction with Schlumpf but no conclusive proof was ever provided. It would appear that Shakespeare took the truth with him to his grave.

Later in the book we show two letters that give an idea of the kind of correspondence Schlumpf and Shakespeare had.

The Shakespeare collection ready to be shipped.
(Photo collection David Gulick)

The Malmerspach collection

In addition to the collection in the official museum in Mulhouse, Fritz Schlumpf owned a reserve collection in an adjacent building. It consisted mostly of automobiles that needed repairs or restoration before being included in the official collection. The fact that some 40 workers from his factories worked every day on restoring these cars, was held against Schlumpf in one of the court cases. The employees got their salaries from the factories (owned, by the way, by Schlumpf, so what was the problem?). Does it not happen in other companies as well that people work on other things than the core business? Does this not happen in civil service also, even in France? Does a company's owner not have the right to ask his workers, upon consultation, to do other jobs? Is he not the one who provides the capital that allows the company to function, and is he not the one who runs all the risks? All of this shows on what low level the matter was being dealt with in the 1970s and '80s, because what difference did 40 workers actually make on a total of more than 2000?

Additionally, there was another reserve collection, consisting of 68 vehicles for which there was no room in the Mulhouse building while they were waiting for their turn to be restored. Fritz put them in storage in Malmerspach, in Alsace, where he resided in a large

Italian pride: Lancia Astura with Pinin Farina body in the Malmerspach collection. (Photo collection Christian Huet)

A BMW Veritas Rennsport Spyder next to a Bugatti T57 Galibier. (Photo collection Christian Huet)

villa and where many of the workers also lived. When the French government confiscated the Schlumpf collection, the automobiles in Malmerspach were, of course, seized as well. Next, these often valuable cars were kept in an open storage area, without any form of protection or surveillance, from the late '70s until 1999, when they were returned to Arlette Schlumpf. Needless to say that in the more than 20 years that the French government was responsible for the collection, many parts were stolen – something we were able to verify in 2008. A beautiful Alfa Romeo 6C2300 with Pinin Farina body was even stolen. In 2013, however, this vehicle, which disappeared in the late 1970s, suddenly showed up. Our investigation indicated that it had been thoroughly restored in Italy, but then, unfortunately, we lost track of it again. Because of a special French law the current owner cannot be held accountable for any wrongdoing if, at the time of purchase, he could not know that the vehicle had been stolen. Highly unusual, because in many other European countries the law is different in such cases.

Obviously the collection was in deplorable condition when Arlette Schlumpf got it back in 1999. She put it in storage in Wettolsheim. Unfortunately, there were leaks in the building so that in the nine years during which she owned the collection, its condition got worse. In 2008, just before Arlette's passing, there were contacts with Frenchman Bruno

1936 Bugatti T57 Ventoux awaiting better times.
(Photo collection Christian Huet)

Vendiesse and Dutchman Jaap Braam Ruben about selling the collection to them. A few weeks after her death, the sale was finalised. Next, the most important automobiles in the collection were sold to Peter Mullin for his museum in Oxnard, where initially he put them on display without any restoration. The other vehicles were sold as well, and even the most pitiful among them were restored to their original glory. The most beautiful example is the Lancia Dilambda of 1929, which Gerard Lansink, with incredible patience, was able to rebuild from the wreck it had become into a magnificent automobile, in good driving condition. Another good example is the Bugatti T57C Stelvio that, after some meandering, came to the Van der Meij company in Putten, the Netherlands, where it was restored perfectly, and is now owned by Adrian van der Kroft.

1937 Bugatti T57C Stelvio in Prague for restoration. (Photo collection Jaap Braam Ruben)

A beautiful sight: several Bugatti in the Malmerspach collection just prior to their shipment to the Mullin Museum in the US; because of strict transportation regulations the tyres unfortunately had to be replaced. (Photo collection Op de Weegh)

The beauty of an unrestored automobile.
(Photo collection Dufilho)

Car descriptions

1937 Bugatti T57C Stelvio #57507

This true Frenchman, a real Bugatti T57C Stelvio, was built in Molsheim, where it was equipped with a straight-eight engine (3257cc), with engine number 14C. Experienced Bugatti driver Michel Dovaz once told us that driving a supercharged T57 was a real delight.

On August 10, 1937, the car was ready – that is, the body had been completely built. This was done by Gangloff Coachwork in Colmar. The car is equipped with a so-called Cotal gearbox. Many luxury automobiles in those days (Delage, Bugatti, and Delahaye) had a 'preselector' gearbox. The driver could put the vehicle into the next gear with the gearshift, but the actual shift happened only after depressing the clutch.

This Stelvio remained in France until 1957, when it was sold to John W Shakespeare, who, in addition to different sports, loved French automobiles, especially Bugattis. On March 1, 1964, Fritz Schlumpf paid $4500 to buy this car from Shakespeare, but it was never restored while it was part of the Schlumpf collection. The fact that there were already three Stelvio Cabriolets in the museum collection may have played a role in this. In 2008, Jaap Braam Ruben

The Bugatti T57C in all its splendour. (Photo collection Van der Kroft)

Specifications:	
Engine	eight-cylinder, in-line, 3257cc
Bore x stroke	72 x 100mm
Compression ratio	6.6 : 1
Power	160hp at 4500rpm
Top speed	109mph
Weight	1727kg
Wheelbase	330cm
Front track	135cm
Rear track	135cm
Production year	1936
Number produced	769 (T57)
Price (new)	F fr 85.000

became the owner of this fabulous automobile, and had a Czech company, Classic Centre Prague (Evzen Majoros), start working on its restoration, but it was never completed by that company.

The work on this fabulous car was continued in the Netherlands, where the current owner bought it, by the Van der Meij company, who restored it, with a blue interior and exterior, to original standards. Currently, the car is looking better than new, and appears exactly as Ettore Bugatti would have wanted.

In late 2016, the current owner got a Dutch licence plate so that its beauty can now grace roads in the Netherlands.

The Bugatti T57C Stelvio while in the Malmerspach collection, late 1970s. (Photo collection Christian Huet)

The T57C Stelvio now is better than new. (Photo collection Van der Kroft)

Left, above & opposite: The T57C Stelvio while being restored by the Van der Meij company.
(Photo collection Op de Weegh)

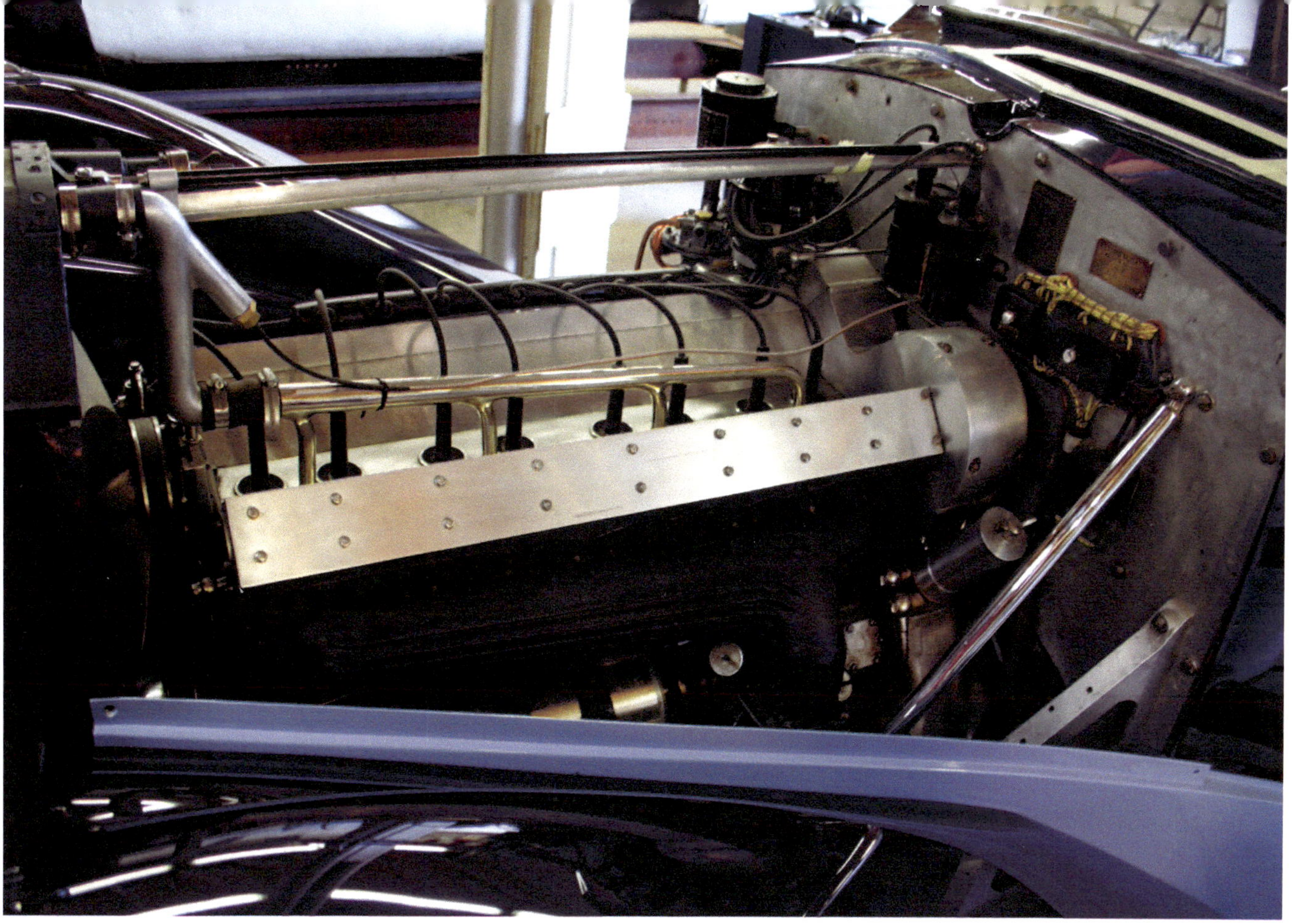

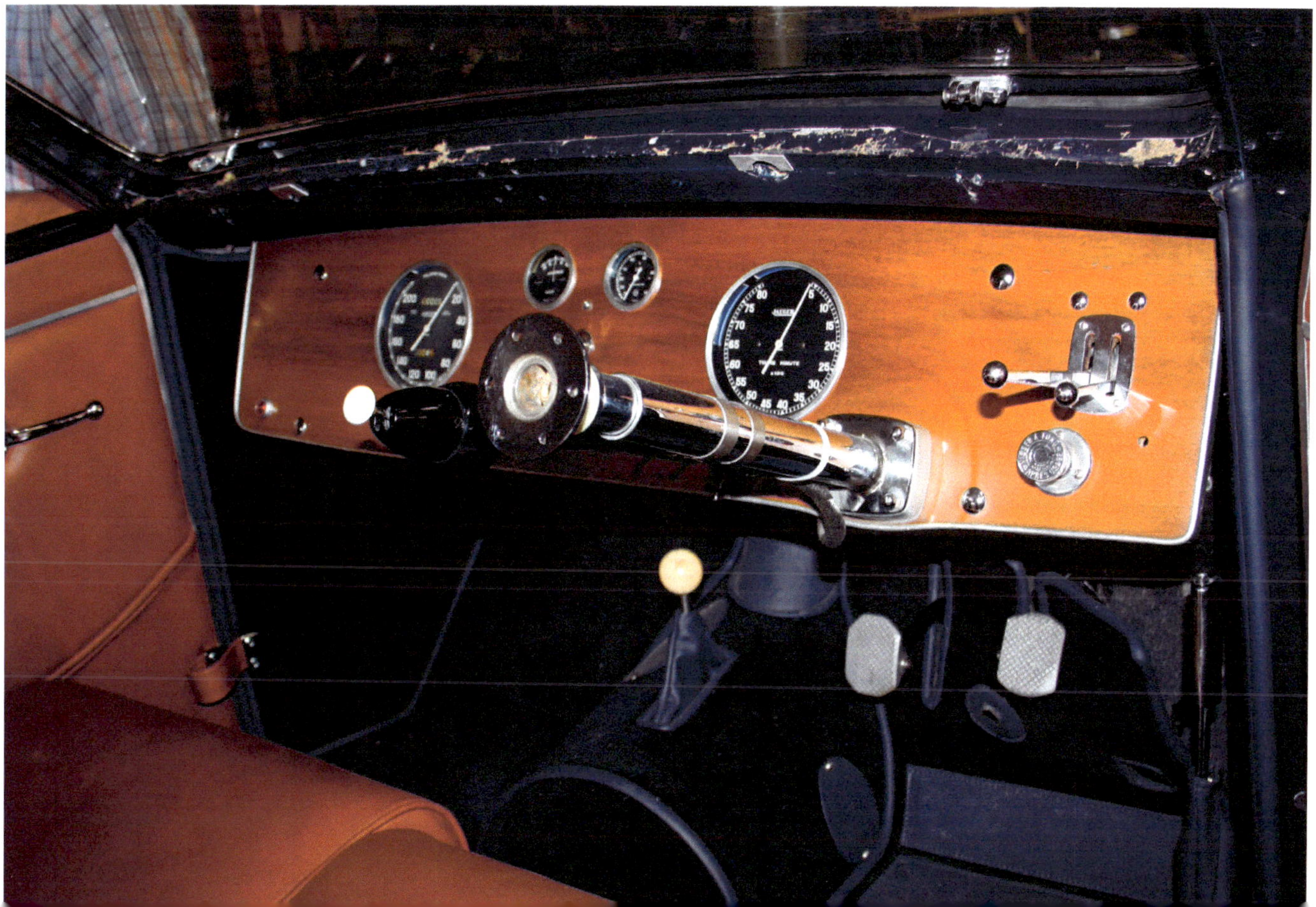

1929 Lancia Dilambda #27-306

The Lancia Dilambda in all its splendour. (Photo collection Op de Weegh)

The Lancia Dilambda was the successor to the Lambda. In contrast to the Lambda it had a 3960cc V8 engine, rather than the 2568cc V4, and was equipped with a body-on-frame construction.

The Dilambda made its first appearance on the market in 1929, and was the largest automobile Lancia had built. During its first presentation at the Paris Motor Show it was received enthusiastically. Because of the 100 horsepower generated by the V8, the car was able to reach a speed of 85mph, which, at the time, was an excellent performance. At the same time, the Dilambda was quite comfortable because of its ability to accept fourth gear quickly, which made it very pleasant to drive. For all these reasons the Dilambda was considered to be in the same league as Bugatti and Bentley.

Schlumpf bought this automobile on April 19, 1963, from a certain Mr Eckert, paying him 500 French francs. However, the car was never displayed in the museum and took a significantly different route.

Via Jaap Braam Ruben and Bruno Vendiesse, Gerard Lansink bought the car in 2008, and what happened when he went to France to pick it up is, in itself, rather interesting: the car did not quite fit on the

Specifications:

Engine	eight-cylinder, in V, 3960cc
Bore x stroke	79 x 100mm
Compression ratio	5.25 : 1
Power	100hp at 3800rpm
Top speed	85mph
Weight	2010kg
Wheelbase	348cm
Front track	146cm
Rear track	148cm
Production years	1929-1930
Number produced	1104 (first series)
Price (new)	unknown

trailer but he managed to transport it all the way to the Netherlands anyway, by tilting the car on the trailer.

Putting in several years of hard work, Gerard was able to improve the car's condition significantly, and to obtain a Dutch licence plate for it. After several months the engine was running again, but the double pumper Zenith carburettor failed and broke into a thousand pieces when Gerard began working on it. With the help of two new SU carburettors and a new manifold, Gerard managed to get the engine running properly for the first time since 1963. The odometer shows only 72,000km, which, Gerard believes, might well be correct.

Gerard chose to restore this automobile according to his own specifications and wishes. Thus, he built a completely new body, which he designed himself, modelled after a Lancia racer from the 1930s (which participated in the 1933 Coupe des Alpes Françaises). Gerard had always wanted to build a pre-war race car, and this Dilambda chassis allowed him to realise his dream. The restoration was done splendidly, with a keen eye for detail.

In 2014 we met with Gerard, and by then the automobile had a Dutch licence plate. It was quite a special moment for us to see how well the car had been repaired and restored, and to admire its

The Dilambda's robust back end. (Photo collection Op de Weegh)

condition. We drove the car and, for a while, thought we were back in the 1930s. What an enormous power this four-litre eight-cylinder engine generated. We felt like young boys again!

Thanks to the meticulous restoration and good body choice, this 'Malmerspach automobile' is on the road again.

The Lancia Dilambda during its stay at Bruno Vendiesse's, where Gerard Lansink bought it in 2008. (Photo collection Gerard Lansink)

Above & opposite: beautiful details of a fabulous automobile. (Photo collection Op de Weegh)

The example on which Gerard Lansink based the new body. (Photo collection Op de Weegh)

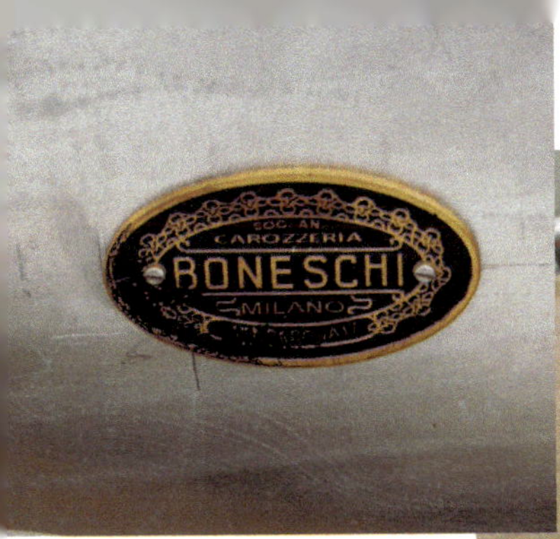
SOC. AN.
CAROZZERIA
BONESCHI
MILANO

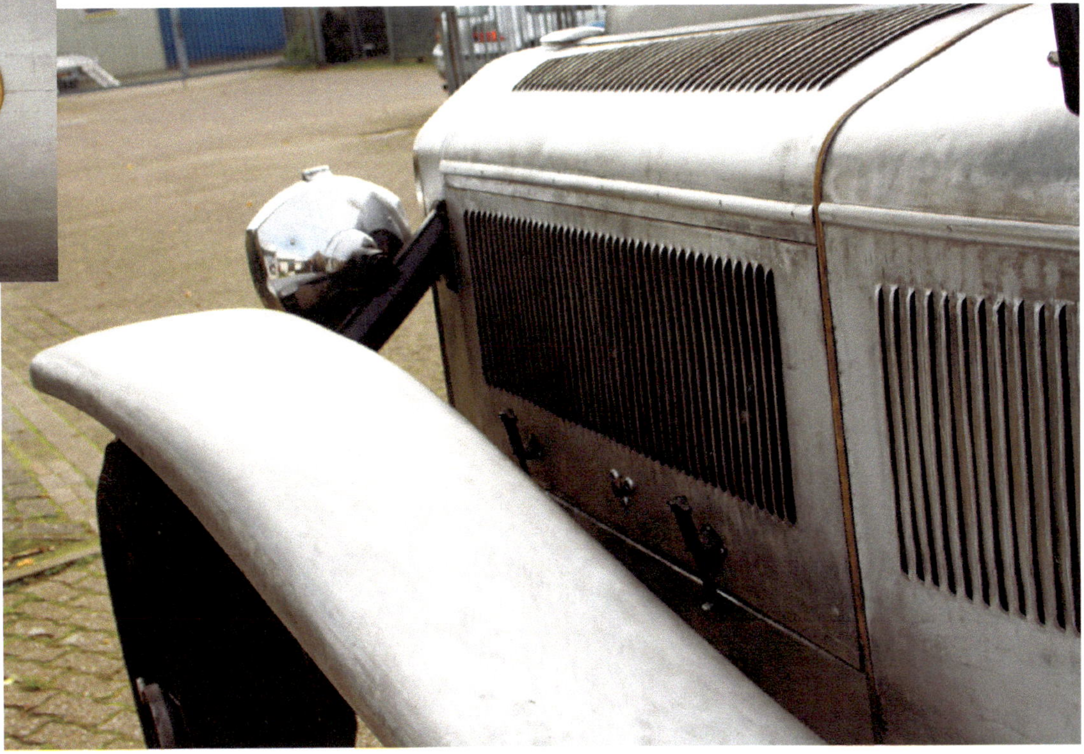

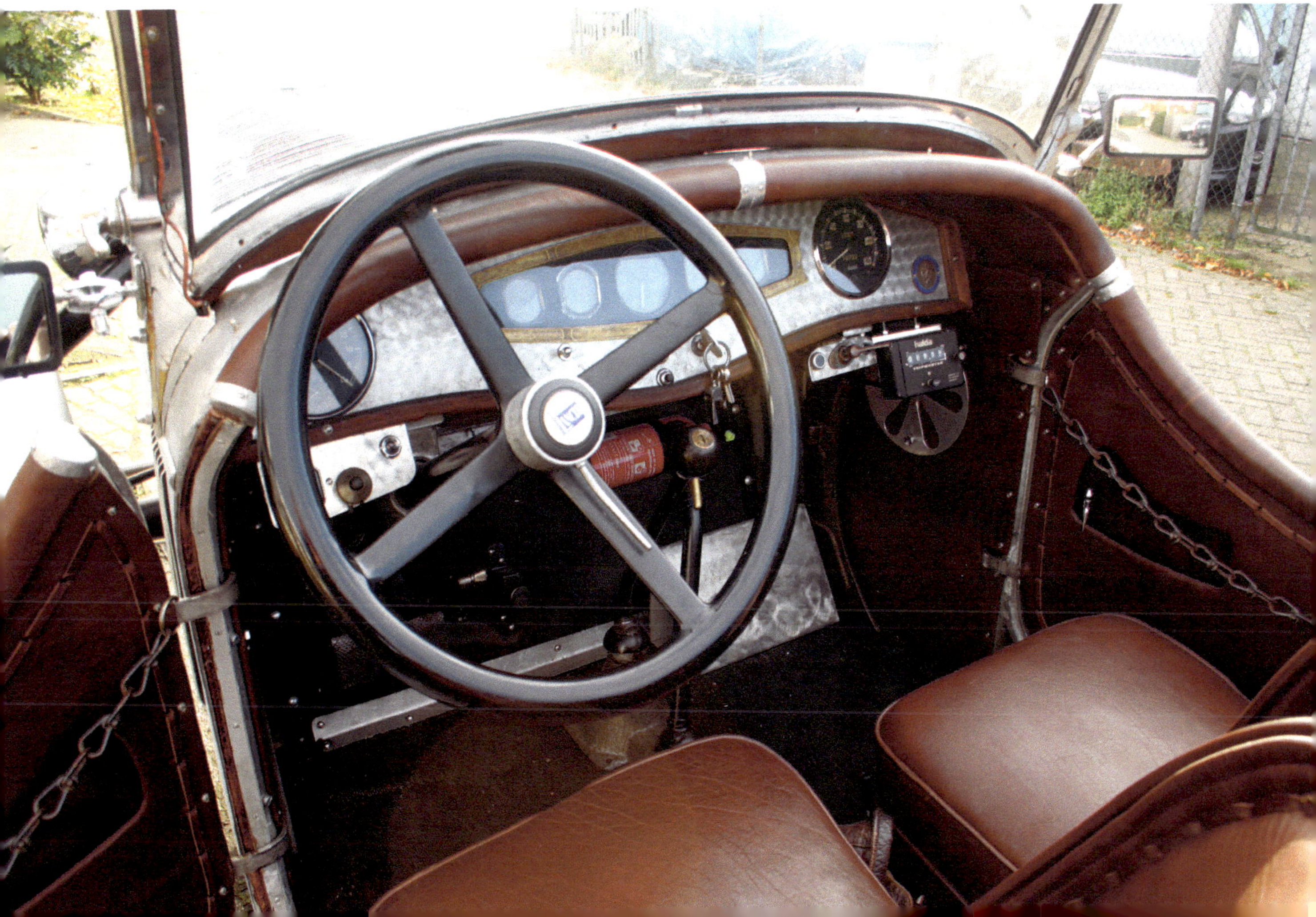

1936 Alfa Romeo 6C2300 B Lungo Pinin Farina
Engine #823106

Alfa Romeo has played a most important role in automobile history. Partly because of its sometimes truly fabulous designs and excellent engine performance, the make proved its quality right from the start.

In 1923 Vittorio Jano went from Fiat to Alfa Romeo, where, between 1924 and 1927, he was responsible for all of the marque's Grand Prix models. He also contributed to designing, amongst others, the 6C and 8C. Since 1925 Alfa Romeo had been building straight-six cars, named 6C. The 6C described here is from 1936, and has the famous six-cylinder engine with a capacity of 2300cc. In 1934 the 6C2300 was built for the first time, the successor to the 6C1900 and the 6C1750. In the first year of production, there were three models in the 2300 series: the Gran Turismo with with a short wheelbase (295cm); the 2300 Pescara (supercharged version) with a short wheelbase (295cm); and the 2300 Lungo with a long wheelbase (321cm).

In 1936 the 6C2300 B made its appearance. Unlike the A model, it had a four-speed gearbox in which the

An Alfa Romeo 6C2300 B Lungo Pinin Farina at the 2013 Rétromobile, with engine number 823106; the same number was found in the official 1977 police reports.

second, third, and fourth gear were fully synchronised. Moreover, the B model had independent suspension on all four wheels. All of this meant much greater comfort.

The car described here (814047, with matching engine number 823106, as various documents show) is a 6C2300 B Lungo with a Pinin Farina body. It was seen for the first time at the 1936 Turin Motor Show, and was built for a German client. Lancia built the chassis in 1935, and Pinin Farina then added the body. Apparently, this type of vehicle also played a role in the 1952 movie *Day for Night*, in which it was driven by Monique Darbaud.

Schlumpf owned this fabulous, Art Deco-style Alfa Romeo for many years, but unfortunately the car did not go to his museum. It was part of the Malmerspach collection. However, a 1997 inspection report by a good friend, Christian Huet, who, between 1972 and 1979 had taken detailed pictures of the vehicles, indicated that the automobile was no longer in the collection.

In 2013 an identical vehicle was offered for sale at the Paris Rétromobile. According to the seller an Italian automobile collector had acquired it in 1996, and had, in the following ten years, brought it back to its 'as new' condition. The engine number was 823106, the same as in 1977 police reports. Moreover, the appraisal documents list chassis number 14047, which is almost identical to the number listed in Paris: 814047.

Specifications:	
Engine	six-cylinder, in-line, 2309cc
Bore x stroke	70 x 100mm
Compression ratio	7,8 : 1
Power	95hp at 4500rpm
Top speed	90mph
Weight	1400kg
Wheelbase	321cm
Front track	144cm
Rear track	146cm
Production year	1936
Number produced	86 (6C2300 B)
Price (new)	unknown

Una vettura espressamente costruita pel mercato tedesco: la trasformabile 4 posti di Pinin Farina su chassis Alfa Romeo 6 c. 2300 B lungo.

Alfa Romeo advertisement in the 1930s.

This page & opposite: the Alfa Romeo while in storage in Malmerspach. (Photo collection Christian Huet)

S. A. *Alfa Romeo* MILANO

TRASFORMABILE "PININ FARINA,, 4 POSTI
SU **6C 2300 B LUNGO** TIPO SALONE DI BERLINO 1938

1936 Lancia Astura Pinin Farina #33-2810

In 1933 Lancia launched a very lavish model, the Astura, named after the peninsula in Lazio. Produced until 1939, it was intended to replace the Lambda and Dilambda, which were luxurious as well as successful.

The Lancia Astura has always been equated with luxury and class. Its success was immediate when it was first presented at the 1931 Paris Motor Show. The most beautiful bodies in the whole world were to be built on it, which is indeed what happened: coachbuilders such as Touring, Pinin Farina, Bertone, and Boneschi produced fabulous models.

The Astura was produced in four series:

Series 1 Type 230:	1931-1932
Series 2 Type 230:	1932-1933
Series 3 Type 233 Lungo:	1933-1937
Series 3 Type 233 Corto:	1933-1936
Series 4 Type 241:	1937-1939

The Astura's V8 was very popular because of its small physical size. This V8 engine is hardly larger than a four-cylinder and, thus, could be installed quite easily (also in the Artena, which was smaller than the Astura). With a capacity of 2604cc this engine generated 73hp, which allowed the car to reach, rather easily, a top speed of 80mph.

The Astura being discussed here (33-2810) is a Series 3 Type 233 Lungo; that is, the third series with a long chassis. The Pinin Farina body gives it a beautiful, elegant look. Classic Skills in the Netherlands is presently working on the car to bring it back, according to the owner's instructions, to pristine condition.

This automobile was purchased by Peter Mullin in 2008, together with (almost) the entire Malmerspach collection. Several years later it came back to Europe and, within the not too distant future, we should be able to admire this gem of the automobile industry on Europe's roads.

After the Schlumpf period this Lancia Astura travelled all over the world; here it is near the Mullin Museum in Oxnard. (Photo collection Mullin Museum USA)

Specifications:	
Engine	eight-cylinder, in V, 2972cc
Bore x stroke	75 x 85mm
Compression ratio	5.35 : 1
Power	82hp at 4000rpm
Top speed	80mph
Weight	1700kg
Wheelbase	333.2cm
Front track	137.4cm
Rear track	139.6cm
Production year	1936
Number produced	1665 (series 3 and 4, all bodies)
Price (new)	unknown

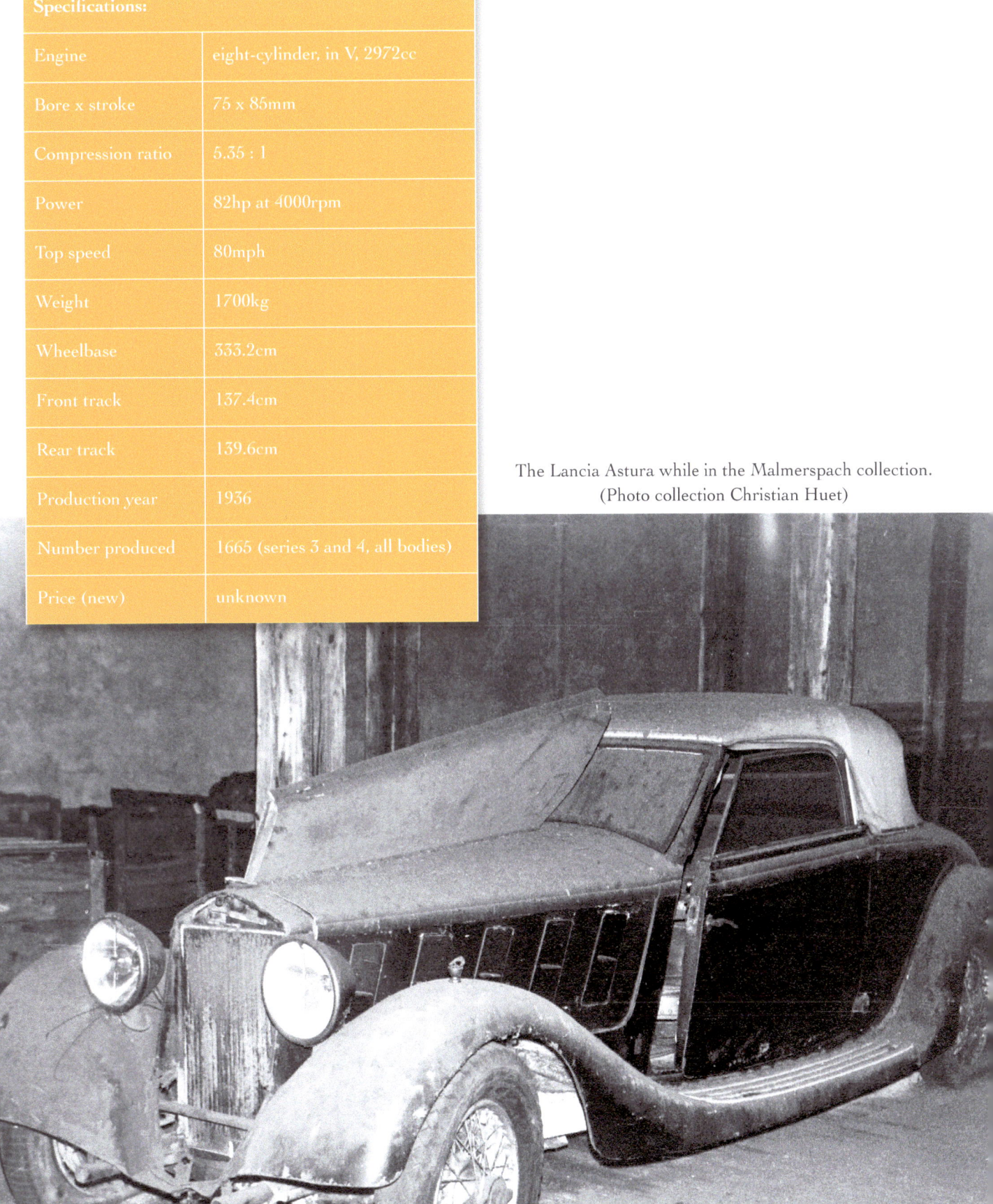

The Lancia Astura while in the Malmerspach collection.
(Photo collection Christian Huet)

The Lancia Astura while in the Mullin Museum in Oxnard. (Photo collection Janssen)

After the Malmerspach period the sheet metal deserved to be repaired. (Photo collection Op de Weegh)

Body being built at Classic Skills; the craftsmanship is evident. (Photo collection Op de Weegh)

Parts of the Astura neatly arranged prior to restoration at Classic Skills. (Photo collection Op de Weegh)

Gorgeous even before restoration. (Photo collection Op de Weegh)

1937 Auto Union Wanderer W25K #180223

The car brand Auto Union was established in 1932, in Germany. This so-called union of Audi, Horch, Wanderer, and DKW was intended to help Germany recover from its economic problems. Four rings, each representing one party, symbolised this union. The rings can still be seen on every modern Audi.

In the 1930s Auto Union had very successful Grand Prix race drivers, such as Bernd Rosemeyer, Tazio Nuvolari and Hans Stuck.

Wanderer's biggest contribution to the union was its straight-six engine, which, by the way, was designed by Ferdinand Porsche. It was a lightweight engine with exchangeable cylinders, made in several capacities ranging from 1.7 to 2.3 litres.

When WWII broke out, the union was discontinued. The factories in Siegmar and Schönau were destroyed and never rebuilt.

The W25 had a six-cylinder in-line engine with a capacity of 1949cc. Its 85hp was quite acceptable in 1936. Equipped with a four-speed gearbox and hydraulic brakes on all four wheels, the car must have been a pleasure to drive.

The W25 was an immediate success. It seemed to

The Wanderer right after being sold in 2008; definitely in need of restoration.
(Photo collection Op de Weegh)

The Wanderer right after being sold in 2008; even without restoration, it's very attractive.
(Photo collection Christian Huet)

Specifications:	
Engine	six-cylinder, in-line, 1949cc
Bore x stroke	70 x 85mm
Compression ratio	6.4 : 1
Power	85hp at 4000rpm
Top speed	90mph
Weight	1000kg
Wheelbase	265cm
Front track	132cm
Rear track	133cm
Production years	1936-1939
Number produced	258
Price (new)	RM7950 (1936)

belong to the luxury category, and 149 vehicles were produced (hand-built) in its first year (1936).

Its style was a mix of American and European influences. The low-cut doors remind one of the BMW 328, while, in other respects, one thinks of American cars. The W25's two-piece windshield was typical of cars from the 1930s.

This 1937 W25K 180223 was in the Malmerspach collection, but is now in Oxnard, in Peter Mullin's collection. At the 2009 Concours d'Élégance in Pebble Beach it was displayed as part of 'Audi: 100 years of excellence.'

Note the truly fascinating way in which the hood is opened. (Photo collection Dufilho)

The Wanderer at the 2009 Pebble Beach show, on one of the most expensive pieces of real estate in the world. (Photo collection Mullin Museum USA)

An extraordinary shot; true beauty from the 1930s. (Photo collection Dufilho)

1937 Bugatti T57 Ventoux #57540

The T57 is one of the few Bugattis not known as a racing car, but it was Bugatti's best-selling model: 769 were produced, often with a striking body.

Jean Bugatti, Ettore's son – just 23 years old when the 'Type 57' project was launched – by and large designed it. The T57 was a striking and especially beautiful automobile.

Before the T57 was launched, there was, for almost every style of car, a different Bugatti model. To reduce costs, Ettore decided that a chassis had to be developed on which several body styles could be built.

At the 1934 launch, the availability of four different types was announced: Ventoux (four-seater, two doors); Stelvio (four-seater, convertible, two doors); Galibier (four-seater, four doors), and Grand Raid (two doors, two-seater, roadster). The T57 turned out to be a great success, and even today most of these vehicles are still owned by automobile enthusiasts.

The Bugatti T57 was ideal for long, fast trips. It had a leaf spring suspension with, initially, a split front axle allowing independent suspension. The engine was basically a straight-eight with a capacity of 3257cc, which routinely generated 135hp – a lot, in those days.

Bugatti T57 Ventoux in 2008, just after the Schlumpf period. (Photo collection Dufilho)

In 1936 two additional, sportier models were launched, the T57C and S. The former had a supercharger and generated 160hp, while the T57S had a shorter chassis, making the car somewhat sportier. There was also a T57SC, with a shorter chassis and a supercharger.

This particular Bugatti T57 Ventoux was built in Molsheim in April 1937, then equipped with a two-door Coach Ventoux body made by Gangloff in Colmar, and delivered to its first owner, Mr Ripert, on May 31, 1937. Ripert paid 70,000 French francs, and later traded the car for a Voisin C24 for 10,000 French francs.

The vehicle had had a succession of owners when Fritz Schlumpf acquired it in 1961. F Sipp sold it to him for 1600 French francs (approximately €270), and Fritz added it to his Malmerspach collection. In 1999 this Bugatti was returned to Arlette Schlumpf, who kept it until her death. In 2008 it was sold to Jaap Braam Ruben and Bruno Vendiesse, who then passed

Specifications:	
Engine	eight-cylinder, in-line, 3257cc
Bore x stroke	72 x 100mm
Compression ratio	6.4 : 1
Power	135hp at 4500rpm
Top speed	90mph
Weight	1500kg
Wheelbase	330cm
Front track	135cm
Rear track	135cm
Production year	1937
Number produced	769 (T57)
Price (new)	70,000 French francs

The Ventoux in the Malmerspach halls awaiting better times. (Photo collection Christian Huet)

This Bugatti's interior has seen better days, but definitely still deserves to be restored.
(Photo collection Op de Weegh)

Magnificent headlight from the 1930s.
(Photo collection Op de Weegh)

The Ventoux while in the Mullin Museum.
(Photo collection Mullin Museum USA)

it on to Peter Mullin. Several years later, Mullin sold this Ventoux, which then came to the Netherlands, and was on display at the 2013 Techno Classica.

Another detail worth mentioning is the original chassis plate, which was probably stolen after the French government confiscated the vehicle. This plate turned up at an auction in 2006 (Ladenburg Auktion Frühling 2006, lot number 2222). When the buyer realised that it probably had been stolen, he returned it to the then owner, Peter Mullin.

Just prior to being sold in 2013. (Photo collection Op de Weegh)

Still without a spare wheel, in 2008.
(Photo collection Op de Weegh)

Unfortunately still without the Bugatti logo.
(Photo collection Op de Weegh)

1937 Cord 812 Supercharged #32122

The Cord 810/812 was, and is, a one of a kind car. Many classic car enthusiasts know this automobile because of its beautiful, strong lines. Designed by Gordon Buehrig, it caused a sensation when introduced in 1935, and was seen as an expression of 'the American Dream.' Easily recognisable because of the large exhaust pipes coming out of the bonnet (hood) sides, the model has sporty looks. According to some, this is one of the most stunning designs of the 1930s.

The Cord 810 was well ahead of its time. The car was futuristic, with front-wheel drive and pop-up headlights (the latter could be adjusted from inside).

In 1935 the 810 was introduced with a V8 engine of 4729cc that generated 125hp. In 1937, the Cord 812 was launched, where the customer could opt for the supercharged engine that generated 170hp, making the car much faster than the 810.

Despite its reliable engine, the car later acquired the reputation of being unreliable, mostly because of its complex gearbox. As a result, only 3000 vehicles were built in 1936 and 1937.

The Malmerspach collection had two Cord automobiles: an 810 from 1935 and an 812 from 1937.

The Cord 812 presently is in better-than-new condition. (Photo collection Hicar, Prague)

Specifications:

Engine	eight-cylinder, in V, 4729cm³
Bore x stroke	88.9 x 95.3mm
Compression ratio	6.5 : 1
Power	175hp at 3600rpm
Top speed	109mph
Weight	1776kg
Wheelbase	335.3cm
Front track	142.2cm
Rear track	154.9cm
Production years	1935-1937 (810/812)
Number produced	3000
Price (new)	unknown

The 812 just prior to restoration; note the body's magnificent design.
(Photo collection Hicar, Prague)

Wonderful 1930s American luxury; because of the many clocks and instruments one has the impression of being in the cockpit of an airplane.
(Photo collection Hicar, Prague)

The 812 just before restoration, showing off the famous 'coffin nose.' (Photo collection Hicar, Prague)

The dashboard prior to restoration; actually in fairly good condition given the fact that the car had not been driven for decades. (Photo collection Hicar, Prague)

Better than new; literally all nuts and bolts were made as new. (Photo collection Hicar, Prague)

Beautiful chromework on this supercharged Cord 812. (Photo collection Hicar, Prague)

Here we discuss the Cord with the supercharged engine.

Fritz Schlumpf bought the 812 (#32122) in 1962 from Truninger. Unfortunately, it was not restored while in the Malmerspach collection, but, when the collection was sold in 2008, Hicar, a Czech automobile company in Prague, bought, among other vehicles, the two Cord cars, and decided to restore them. This was done most carefully, and the result is that the 812 is 'as new,' looks authentic, and can be seen again in all its splendour on Europe's roads.

1936 Maserati 4CM #1526

The Maserati marque has always appealed to the imagination as a symbiosis of art and technology. It was founded in 1914, in Bologna, by six Maserati brothers: Carlo, Bindo, Alfieri, Mario, Ettore, and Ernesto. At first, they produced only sparkplugs and coils. In the late 1920s, the so-called cyclecar challenge for automobiles with relatively small engines was extremely popular among amateur racers, and several marques tried to get a share of the profits. For Maserati, too, there were quite a few opportunities during these years, which the company seized.

In 1926, Maserati launched its first car at the Targa Florio. Driven by Alfieri Maserati, it won. Later, the car won several other races.

Production ended after just four versions of the 8C1100 had been built, the main reason being that the eight-cylinder engine was really too heavy

The Maserati 4CM awaiting better times. (Photo collection Hottendorff)

Specifications:

Engine	four-cylinder, in-line, 1498cc
Bore x stroke	69 x 100mm
Compression ratio	6.0 : 1
Power	140hp at 6000rpm
Top speed	142mph
Weight	470kg
Wheelbase	240cm
Front track	120cm
Rear track	120cm
Production years	1934-1938
Number produced	12
Price (new)	unknown

for these cars. To be competitive again, the marque then developed the first four-cylinder engine for its racing car. Equipped with a double overhead camshaft and a supercharger, the new engine, with a capacity of 1088cc, generated 90hp. This capacity was comparable to that of the earlier eight-cylinder, but with a much lower weight – clearly a good choice.

The first 4CTR series was introduced in 1931, and just one car was built. A highlight was its 'best in its class' (1000cc) result in the 1932 Mille Miglia, but the fact that this automobile was the prototype for two new Maserati race cars was actually more important.

The 4CS1100 succeeded the 4CTR and was very similar to its predecessor. Only six vehicles were made. The 4CM1100 was more popular, not only in showrooms as a two-seater sports car but as a monoposto on racetracks as well. Because of its narrower and shorter chassis it was very responsive.

Weighing 470kg and generating a maximum

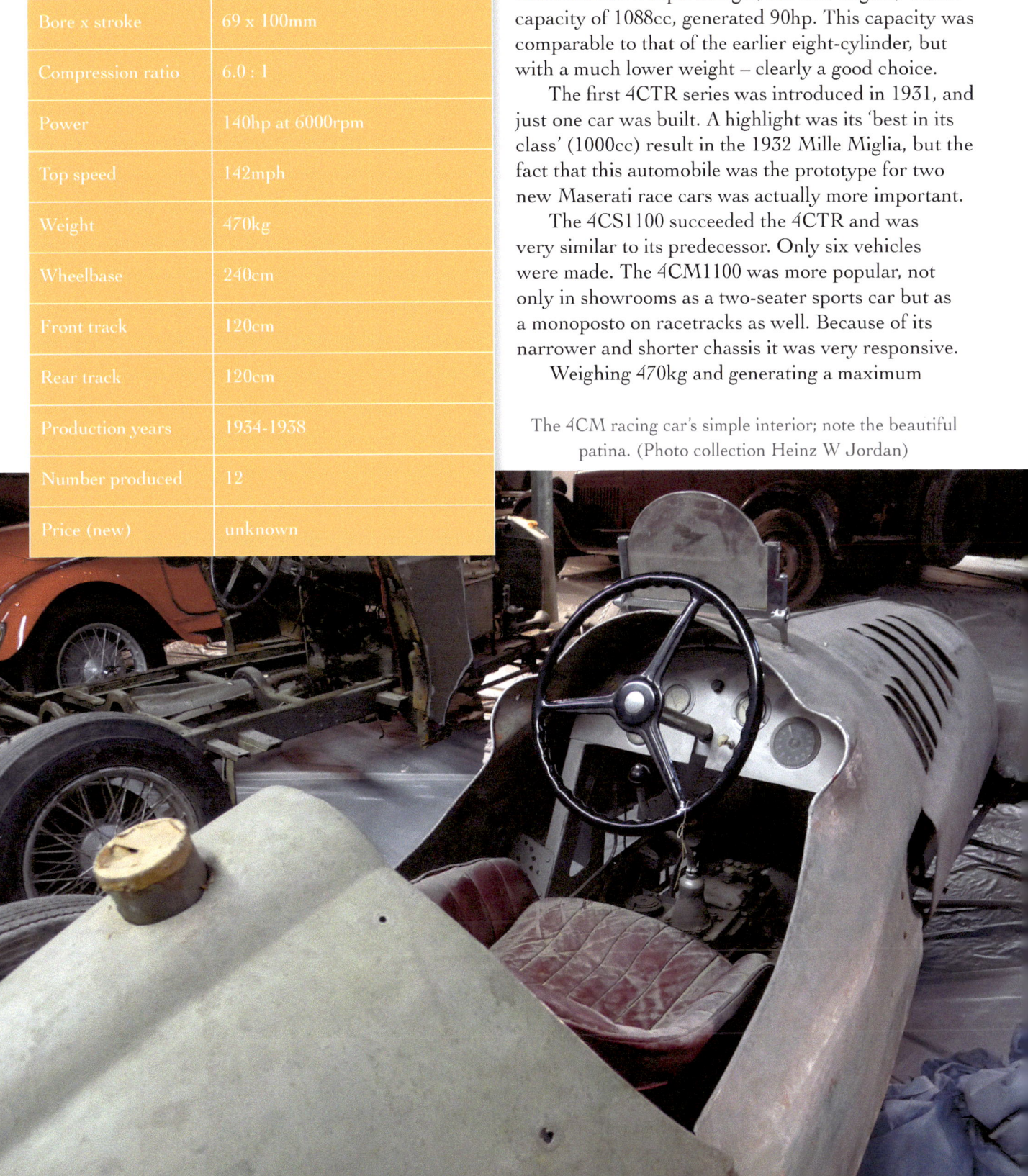

The 4CM racing car's simple interior; note the beautiful patina. (Photo collection Heinz W Jordan)

Right now this true race car is completely worn out, which is especially noticeable in its tyres.
(Photo collection Jeroen Vossen)

150hp, this 4CM was a true racer, and obtained numerous successes. The Schlumpf brothers purchased #1526 in 1963 for just 2500 French francs, which today looks like a ridiculously small sum. Even though a vehicle of this class and with such a rich history would have deserved restoration, this has never happened. Today, the car is in a deplorable condition, and seeing it in such bad shape will probably bring tears to the eyes of those who love this characteristic Italian marque. It is to be hoped that the future will be kinder to this Maserati, and that eventually it will be seen again on the racetrack.

Will this Maserati ever again be seen on a racetrack? (Photo collection Heinz W Jordan)

1939 Mercedes-Benz W154 Silver Arrow #189436

The Mercedes-Benz W154 is without any doubt one of the most beautiful vehicles in the Schlumpf brothers' museum reserve collection. Because of its extraordinary appearance it is a true eye-catcher that makes many a heart beat faster.

Soon after the first official car races were held, rules and regulations were imposed. One of these, applied between 1934 and 1936 to Grand Prix races, meant that cars could not exceed 750kg. This was the only restriction. In all other respects, designers and engineers had free rein. No wonder this resulted in bigger, more powerful engines on light chassis; but these cars were not safe. Mercedes-Benz was a dominant presence in those days with the wonderful W125, which had a power output of 592hp and hardly any protection against accidents. It had a 12-cylinder engine with a capacity of 5576cc.

In order to reduce the number of accidents, some restrictions were imposed in 1937. These were based on engine capacity. A minimum weight in each of two categories was required, and the category choice was between a three-litre engine with supercharger or a normally-aspirated four-litre engine.

Opting for the three-litre supercharged engine, which it expected to have a more solid future than the other type, Mercedes launched the W154 in 1938. This car was nicknamed 'Silberpfeil' (Silver Arrow) because of its striking grey colour and its incredible speed.

Compared to the W125, the W154 had many

There was a time when this W154 dominated Europe's racetracks. (Photo collection Jeroen Vossen)

advantages. The wheelbase was shorter, which was facilitated by the smaller engine. Furthermore, independent suspension was introduced, making the car a lot safer.

After engine choice, weight remained a very important factor. To achieve a lower weight, several holes were cut in the chassis. The W154's new three-litre engine had four valves per cylinder. Two superchargers were installed on the block's front end. All in all, it was a good, strong engine.

Unfortunately, only 14 chassis were built for the W154, and 19 engines. Famous racers such as Rudolf Caracciola, Manfred von Brauchitsch, and Hermann Lang, drove these cars.

At the present time at least nine W154 automobiles are still known to exist. The one from the Schlumpfs' museum reserve collection has chassis number #189436, and was purchased in 1966 for 14,000 Swiss francs, which today is a pittance for such a car. If ever it is put on the market, millions will be paid for it, which we think it eminently deserves.

Specifications:

Engine	12-cylinder, in V, 2962cc
Bore x stroke	67 x 70mm
Compression ratio	7.5 : 1
Power	480hp at 7800rpm
Top speed	192mph
Weight	1727kg
Wheelbase	272.5cm
Front track	147.5cm
Rear track	140cm
Production years	1938-1939
Number produced	14
Price (new)	unknown

This car does not look bad at all.
(Photo collection Heinz W Jordan)

This large 12-cylinder engine dominates the
Mercedes-Benz W154.
(Photo collection Heinz W Jordan)

1929 Bugatti T35B #4933

In the early 1930s Ettore Bugatti already had an excellent reputation in racing circles. He drew a lot of attention both for his designs and the technical aspects of his cars.

Until 1921 Bugatti cars had four-cylinder engines, but this changed when a straight-eight engine was developed, with a capacity of 1991cc. To do this, Bugatti applied what he had learned from the development of airplane engines for the Allies in WWI.

The first model equipped with this new engine was the T32, also known as the 'tank.' When it participated in the 1922 French Grand Prix, it finished in third place. However, Ettore Bugatti was not satisfied with the car, and started designing a new one. His goal was to build a car that any and every amateur race driver, all over the world, could drive, not only during races but on any street. The result was the T35. Its design, performance, and technical aspects were absolutely fabulous, and the T35 should be seen as one of the most, if not the most, successful automobiles in racing history.

The T35B presently occupies a special spot in the Schlumpf museum: right next to the photograph of the Schlumpfs' mother. (Photo collection Op de Weegh)

Specifications:

Engine	eight-cylinder, in-line, 2261cc
Bore x stroke	60 x 100mm
Compression ratio	unknown
Power	125hp at 5500rpm
Top speed	119mph
Weight	750kg
Wheelbase	240cm
Front track	120cm
Rear track	120cm
Production years	1926-1931
Number produced	258
Price (new)	F fr 155.000 (1930)

The T35B's dashboard and easily recognisable wheel – when designing this car, Ettore paid attention to every detail.
(Photo collection Op de Weegh)

Fritz Schlumpf at the wheel of this true race car during one of the races in which he participated.
(Photo collection Patenostre)

Every detail shows that this is a pure-bred race car, and reflects Ettore Bugatti's perfectionism. The aluminum wheels are an excellent example and make the car stand out from other marques.

The T35 discussed here was one of Fritz Schlumpf's favourite automobiles. He drove it several times. The car's story began in 1929 when Bugatti produced it. Its first Grand Prix (in France) was on June 30, 1929. Conelli (#30) was the driver, and finished third.

This T35 is a heavier model than the original. The T35B had a supercharger and the engine's capacity was increased to 2261cc. Its 120hp power makes the car a true racer. Because it weighs just 750kg, it's still competitive in today's oldtimer races.

The easily recognisable T35 wheels.
(Photo collection Op de Weegh)

The T35B in special surroundings in the museum.
(Photo collection Op de Weegh)

Fritz Schlumpf, 'Le Patron,' at the wheel.
(Photo collection Patenostre)

Right & below: #4933 presently is in excellent condition, maybe ready to participate again in races?
(Photo collection Op de Weegh)

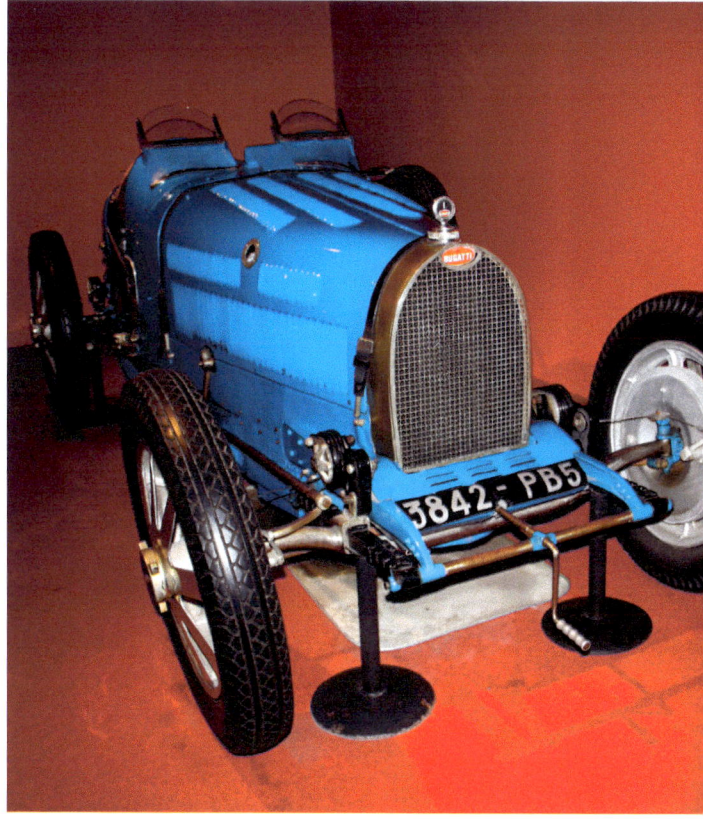

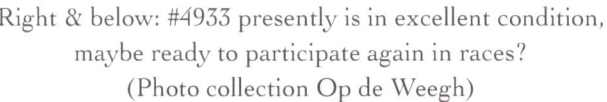

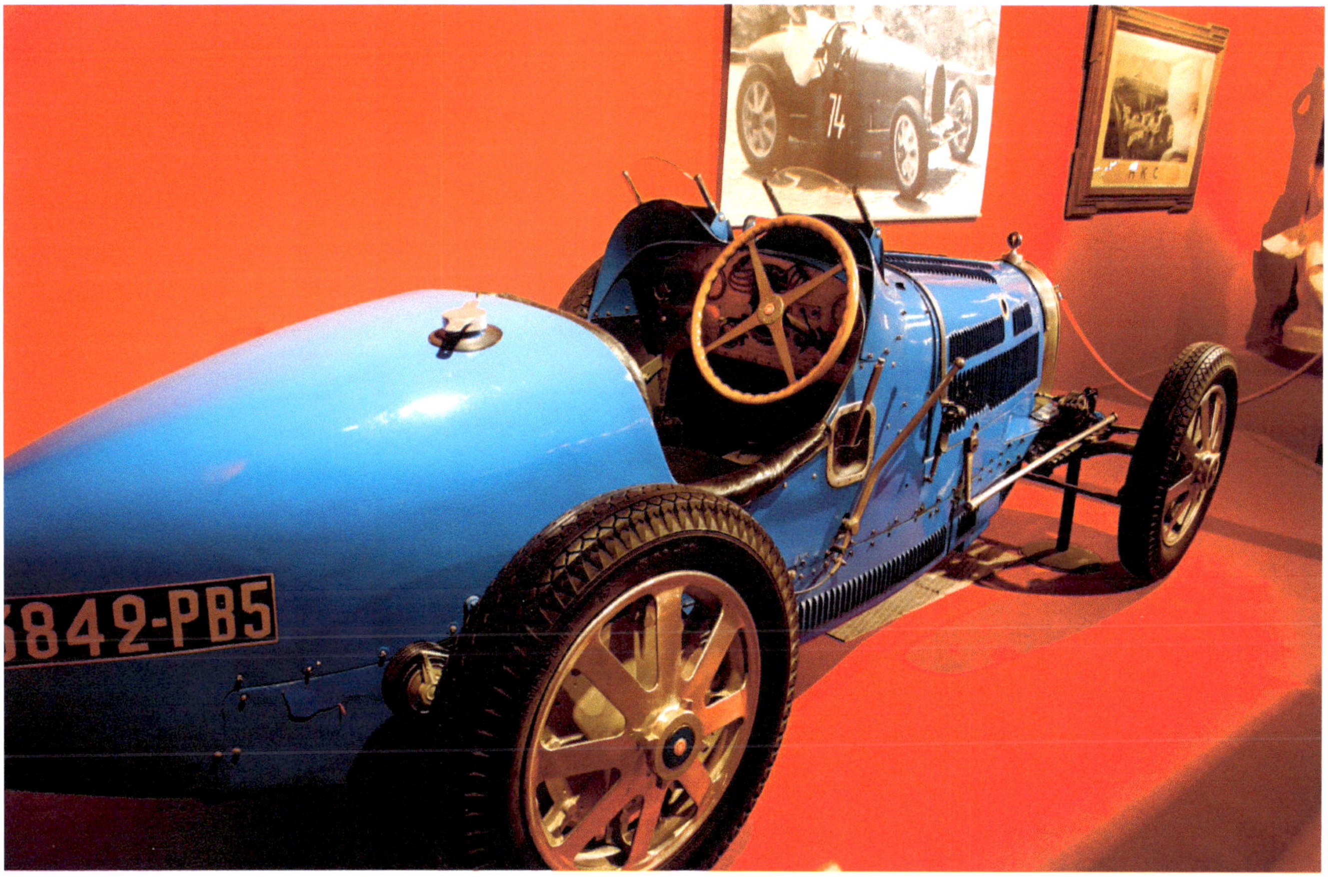

1933 Bugatti T41 Royale Park Ward #41131

The Bugatti T41, better known as Royale, is, perhaps, one of the most famous Bugattis. At the same time it is one of the rarest, as only seven were made (actually, whether it was six or seven is still being debated).

In the 1920s Ettore Bugatti decided to produce this magnificent automobile specifically for members of royal families. He intended to build 25 but stopped at seven because, during the economic crisis in the 1920s, even royals did not buy such expensive automobiles. Ettore ended up selling only three T41 Royales between 1926 and 1933.

Today, the Bugatti Royale should almost be considered the holy grail of car collecting.

The T41 has a 12.7-litre straight-eight engine that allowed the almost-3200kg automobile to reach a top speed of 109mph because of its 275 horsepower. All T41 Bugattis have this engine, except for the first type (#41100, Ettore's personal car until 1963), which has a 14.7-litre engine.

The eight-cylinder engine has three valves per cylinder, operated by a centrally-located, single overhead camshaft. The engine's design was based on that of an airplane for the French Air Ministry, which, however, never made it into production.

The T41 had a substantial chassis, with

This gem of the automobile industry displays its beauty in a wonderful spot in the Schlumpf collection.
(Photo collection Op de Weegh)

Specifications	
Engine	eight-cylinder, in-line, 12,763cc
Bore x stroke	125 x 130mm
Compression ratio	4.92 : 5.91
Power	275hp at 3000rpm
Top speed	109mph
Weight	3175kg
Wheelbase	429cm
Front track	160cm
Rear track	160cm
Production years	1926-1933
Number produced	6 (or 7)
Price (new)	unknown

conventional semi-elliptic leaf springs in front. To bring the car to a halt, it was equipped with large brake shoes, mechanically operated by cables. The brakes functioned well, but the driver had to work hard to stop the Royale quickly.

In Mulhouse there are currently three Bugatti T41s:

– 41100 Coupé Napoléon
– 41131 Park Ward Limousine
– 41 Replica Esders

Chassis 41131 (the fourth Royale), which is being discussed here, was sold in 1933 to the English Captain, Cuthbert W Foster, heir to a large department store in Boston, United States. Foster had asked the British coachbuilder Park Ward to design the body for a limousine in the style of a 1921 Daimler. Before the vehicle was delivered, Jean, Ettore Bugatti's son, travelled to London to place the elephant mascot on the radiator and to start the engine.

In 1947, the British Bugatti dealer Jack Lemon Burton bought this automobile from Foster for approximately $2800 and kept it for ten years. In June/July 1956 it was sold, in perfect condition, to

Picture taken in 1977, right after the takeover by workers. (Photo collection Op de Weegh)

The beautiful Bugatti Royale's ornament.
(Photo collection Op de Weegh)

John Shakespeare, becoming part of the then largest collection of Bugattis. Shakespeare paid $9785, which was a hefty price, and in 1964 sold his entire collection to Fritz Schlumpf, who was eager to get it.

The Royale's simple yet sophisticated dashboard.
(Photo collection Op de Weegh)

The Royale's magnificent design is a pleasure to look at.
(Photo collection Op de Weegh)

The Royale's interior reflects late-1920s luxury.
(Photo collection Op de Weegh)

The Bugatti Royale's characteristic wheels.
(Photo collection Op de Weegh)

The T41 Royale's impressive front end.
(Photo collection Op de Weegh)

1953 Ferrari 250MM #0230MM

Mass production is definitely not a term associated with Ferrari automobiles of the early 1950s. Ferrari provided the chassis and the engines, and various Italian companies designed the bodies. The first Ferrari in the 250 series was the 250S, built in 1952, and available in two models: the Berlinetta and the Spider. Its successor, the 250MM, appeared the following year. At the same time, another model was presented, intended for export, with a longer wheelbase and, therefore, a larger interior. The Ferrari 250 is highly sought-after by collectors today, and, in the past few years, these cars have commanded very high prices at auction.

The car being discussed here is the Ferrari 250MM, with series number 0230MM. Its first buyer, in 1953, was Roberto Rossellini (famous in the movie industry), who immediately drove the car in the Mille Miglia. It had a Vignale body, which, in 1955, was replaced by a Scaglietti body.

Schlumpf purchased this automobile in 1963 from Eckert. Over the years its value has increased enormously.

The race car par excellence in the Mulhouse museum. (Photo collection Op de Weegh)

Specifications:	
Engine	12-cylinder, in V, 2953cc
Bore x stroke	73 x 58.8mm
Compression ratio	9.0 : 1
Power	240hp at 7200rpm
Top speed	155mph
Weight	950kg
Wheelbase	240cm
Front track	132.5cm
Rear track	132cm
Production years	1953-1954
Number produced	31
Price (new)	unknown

#230mm during the 1953 Mille Miglia.

Magnificent design. (Photo collection Op de Weegh)

In reasonable shape in Mulhouse; but to return this race car to pristine condition, it will need a new coat of paint.
(Photo collection Op de Weegh)

The airbox makes this 250MM look very aggresive.
(Photo collection Op de Weegh)

1955 Gordini T32 F1 #42

Within the Schlumpf Museum the Gordini collection is quite unique. Besides Bugattis, Fritz very much liked the Gordini brand. The marque produced a total of 50 automobiles, and Fritz bought 14, all directly from Gordini in 1964, with the exception of one 26S, which he got in 1968.

The marque's founder, Amadeo Gordini, was born in 1899 in Bazzano, near Bologna. At a young age he became fascinated by technology, in contrast to his father, who was a horse-trader.

At age 25 Amadeo moved to Paris, a life-changing experience. He became Amédée, and started his career at the famous Hispano-Suiza company, where he gained a great deal of experience in the automotive business.

Young Gordini was ambitious, and, two years later, started his own garage in Paris, where he primarily repaired Fiat cars, and became very interested in racing. He sharpened his knowledge of racing cars and, soon started participating in the Le Mans races. Even though he was rather successful in these competitions, the winnings were not enough to provide a living.

In the mid-1930s Gordini had developed so much knowledge and experience that several car makers took note. In 1934 he signed a contract with the French car marque Simca.

The Gordini T32 at the 2016 Rétromobile. (Photo collection Op de Weegh)

Specifications:	
Engine	eight-cylinder, in-line, 2498cc
Bore x stroke	75 x 70mm
Compression ratio	10.8 : 1
Power	256hp at 7300rpm
Top speed	161mph
Weight	650kg
Wheelbase	230cm
Front track	124cm
Rear track	121.6cm
Production years	1955-1957
Number produced	2
Price (new)	unknown

One result of this collaboration was that six Simca-Gordini automobiles participated in the 1938 Le Mans race, where they made an excellent debut. Gordini's name was established; the French journalist Charles Faroux even called his work 'magic.'

In 1951, the Simca-Gordini collaboration ended and Gordini continued on his own. He opened a workshop on Boulevard Victor in Paris. One of the reasons for the break-up was Simca's refusal to continue to finance F1 races after four Gordini vehicles had retired in the 1951 Le Mans race. For a small company it was extremely hard to compete with other makes that were winning a lot of prizes. Gordini often had to save on the quality of parts, which had an impact on racing results. He did not give up, though, and, as an independent marque, developed a 1987cc engine with a double overhead camshaft. Equipped with three Weber carburettors, this engine generated 175hp.

In 1964 Gordini designed a three-litre, straight-eight engine which was actually based on a

The T32 together with other racers: a fabulous display in Mulhouse. (Photo collection Op de Weegh)

A pure delight, this Gordini F1 Racer. (Photo collection Op de Weegh)

doubled-up version of his earlier 1500cc engine. Equipped with a double overhead camshaft and four Weber carburettors, it managed to generate 235hp.

For the 1955 Formula 1 Amédée developed the Gordini 32. This car, with an eight-cylinder engine of 2498cc, generated 256hp. It was based on the 1954 model, but further developed.

In 1956, when he ended all relations with Simca, Gordini experienced great financial difficulties, and was forced to stop all his business activities for a while. However, it was not long thereafter that Renault associated itself with his marque and appointed Gordini as head of its racing division.

The T32 discussed here carries number 42, and is one of the most exclusive automobiles in the Schlumpf collection. It won several races in its time and is in pristine condition. If it were to appear again on racetracks, it would, we believe, cause a great deal of excitement amongst motor racing fans.

Opposite: the Gordini T32 right after the workers' takeover in 1977. (Photo collection Op de Weegh)

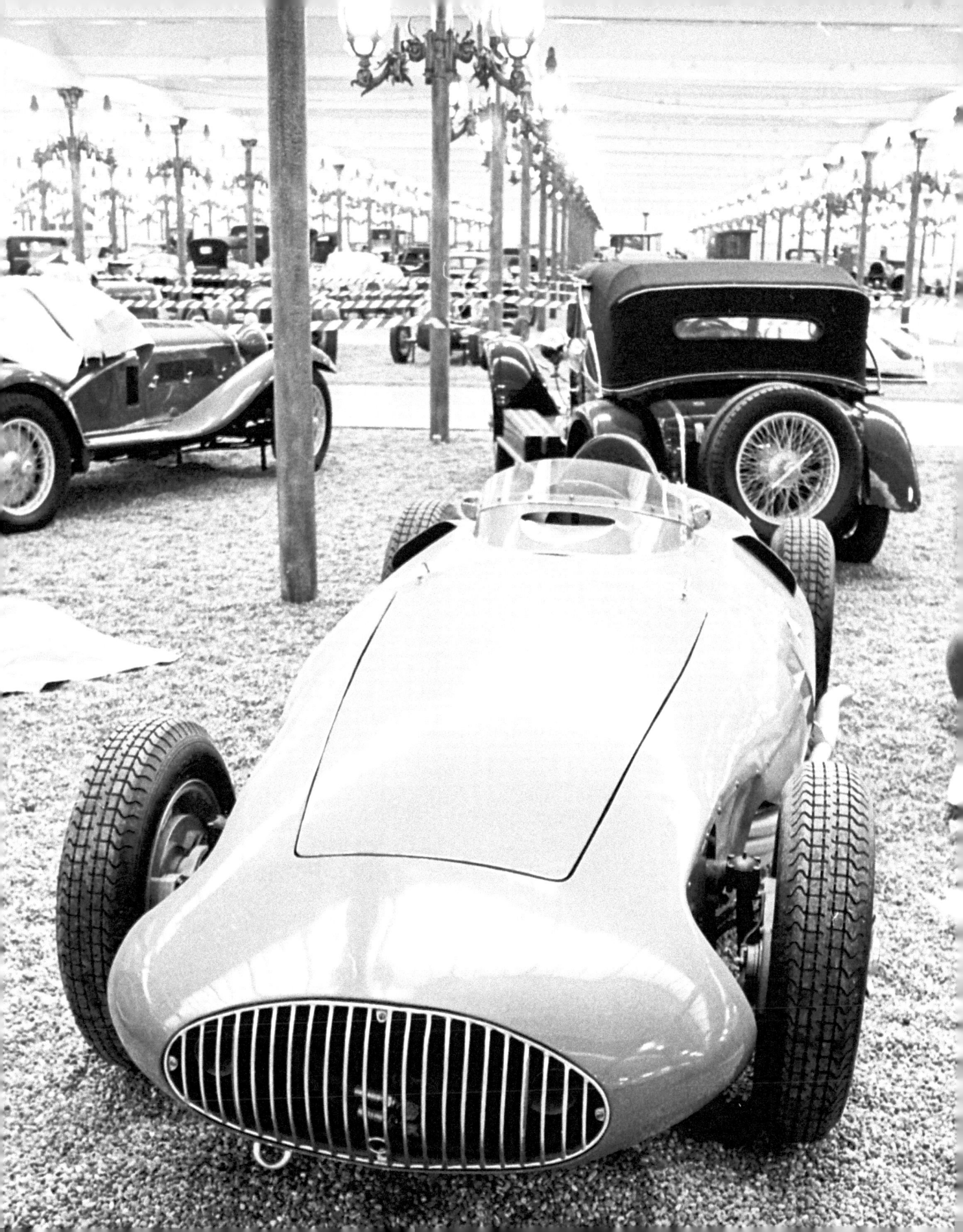

1936 Alfa Romeo 8C2900A Pinin Farina #412004

In the 1930s a good supply of racing cars was available. On the one hand, there were light cars with a lot of horsepower, like the MGs – small, inexpensive, manoeuvrable, and reasonably well-finished. On the other hand, there were luxury automobiles, such as Duesenburgs, Mercedes-Benz 540Ks, and Bentleys, which were fast but heavy. In those days only a handful of cars were luxurious, fast, manoeuvrable, *and* elegant. Bugatti and Alfa Romeo models immediately come to mind.

The Alfa Romeo 8C was first introduced in 1931 as 8C2300, and was intended to succeed the successful 6C1750. At its launch the 8C was not available for private clients, but, in the autumn of the same year, that situation changed. One could opt for a short (Corto) or long (Lungo) wheelbase, and have the body added by an Italian coachbuilder. At the time, Zagato, Touring, Castagna, Pinin Farina, and Brianza were well-known coachbuilders in Italy. Later, clients could also select from bodies made by Graber, Worblaufen, and Tuscher.

The 8C2300's engine, designed by Vittorio Jano, was a straight-eight with a volume of 2336cc. Both the short- and the long-wheelbase models were equipped with this engine, which was able to produce a top speed of 139mph because of its 180hp.

You either love or hate this 8C2900A's design. (Photo collection Op de Weegh)

Specifications:	
Engine	eight-cylinder, in-line, 2905cc
Bore x stroke	68 x 100mm
Compression ratio	6.5:1
Power	220hp at 5300rpm
Top speed	139mph
Weight	unknown
Wheelbase	275cm
Front track	135cm
Rear track	135cm
Production years	1936
Number produced	10 (8C2900A)
Price (new)	unknown

In 1935 the successor, the 8C2900, was launched. First presented at the London Motor Show, it was welcomed by a most enthusiastic audience. The new model had the same engine as the 8C2300, but with an increased capacity of 2905cc. It also was a more luxurious car. Built on an 8C35 Grand Prix chassis, the vehicle was to participate in important rallies, such as the Mille Miglia.

In 1936 Scuderia Ferrari entered the Mille Miglia with three Alfa Romeo 8C2900A cars. Its drivers finished first (Antonio Brivio), second (Giuseppe Farina), and third (Carlo Pintacuda).

The automobile discussed here is the 8C2900A, with series number 412004. In 1936 it participated in the Mille Miglia with a 'Botticelli' body. Apparently, it won first place with driver Antonio Brivio, but we have not been able to verify this 100 per cent. It is a fact, though, that, in 1939, the car was rebuilt with a Pinin Farina body, and, after the war, got yet another completely different body, designed by Martin.

8C2900A in the 1955 Mille Miglia; probably the automobile here described.

Presently, this automobile occupies a prominent position in the museum, as it should. It has both a very rich history and a beautiful, futuristic body.

Alfa Romeo logo typical of this period. (Photo collection Op de Weegh)

1955 Mercedes-Benz 300 SL Gull Wing #5500732

Before WWII Mercedes-Benz was extremely successful in racing. The technology developed by this marque, which was subsidised by the German government, was, at the time, number one on the racetracks. In 1946, however, Germany was a completely different country – one with enormous financial problems. Obviously, no funds were available to stimulate new developments in car racing.

Mercedes-Benz had to re-invent itself, which meant that the company began building practical passenger cars. From the beginning, one of its core values had always been an emphasis on building technically superior, luxurious, high-quality automobiles. The first post-war models can hardly be considered technological marvels; yet, the famous quality was there. Model 170, which was first launched in 1931, sold particularly well. It had a four-cylinder flathead engine.

Within a few years there was room again for what might be called more decadent luxury, resulting in the Mercedes-Benz 300 limousine. Later that year the 220 series was introduced, with a smaller six-cylinder engine. Although it shared some construction details

Arlette Schlumpf's favourite car beautifully displayed in Mulhouse. (Photo collection Op de Weegh)

Specifications:

Engine	six cylinder, in-line, 2996cc
Bore x stroke	85 x 88mm
Compression ratio	8.55 : 1
Power	215hp at 5800rpm
Top speed	149mph
Weight	1293kg
Wheelbase	240cm
Front track	138.4cm
Rear track	143.5cm
Production year	1955
Number produced	1400 (Gull Wing)
Price (new)	DM 29,000

with the larger, three-litre, six-cylinder engine, it nevertheless was very different.

The Wirtschaftswunder was working at full capacity. A Mercedes-Benz factory team even entered the 1952 Monte Carlo Rally and won the team prize. This was the company's first step back into the racing world, but participation in Grand Prix races still was too big a move. The engine designed for the 300 models (M186) was a powerful 2996cc V6. What was striking was the fact that the sparkplugs were mounted in the engine block itself. In series production the six-cylinder engine generated 116hp at 4600rpm, but modified for racing this increased to 175hp.

In 1952 a new type of Mercedes-Benz entered the Mille Miglia race – the so-called W194, but better known as the 300SL, SL standing for 'Sport Leicht.' Its chassis was a space frame construction, consisting

The car presently is in excellent condition.
(Photo collection Op de Weegh)

of welded steel tubes. To make it more solid, its sills (rockers) were very deep. Regular doors would not have provided enough room to enter the car; so the characteristic top-hinged doors were designed. The first 300SL was named 'Gull Wing' precisely because of its special doors. At the request of the US importer the 300SL became available to the general public in 1954, and, between 1954 and 1957, 1400 examples of the 300SL Coupé (Gull Wing) model were sold.

In 1957 a roadster was launched, a choice that was influenced by the US importer. Production of the Gull Wing came to a halt. Especially in California where many Gull Wings had been sold, but, because of the warm climate, there were many complaints. The limited ventilation easily led to high temperatures inside the car. Getting into the car was also a bit difficult, and people's desire to have greater comfort and accessability led to the design of the magnificent Roadster.

Neither the Gull Wing nor the Roadster was fuel-efficient, but, because fuel prices were quite a bit lower in those days, it did not really matter. While the Gull Wing had a 130-litre fuel tank, the one in the Roadster had a capacity of 'only' 100 litres. Both models had a manual four-speed gearbox. A striking feature was the direct fuel injection, a novelty for a petrol (gasoline) engine in a passenger car!

In the Schlumpf museum one can also admire a 300SL made in 1955. This is not just any car – it was Arlette Schlumpf's favourite, but in the museum this fact has not received any special attention. It does occupy a prominent place, though – which an automobile of this kind definitely deserves.

In summer the 300SL Gull Wing can often be seen with its doors wide open; cooling the car's interior was problematic. (Photo collection Op de Weegh)

About the authors

Since childhood, Arnoud has been crazy about automobiles. When he could barely walk there was nothing he enjoyed more than to accompany his dad to the garage to smell that mix of oil and petrol associated with cars. When Arnoud was a little older and discovered that his dad had truly interesting books about classic automobiles, his love of these vehicles was born. Father and son have visited (and still visit) many automobile shows all over Europe, and their knowledge and networks have grown along the way.

Together with Kay Hottendorff, father and son wrote their first book, *Het lot van de Slapende Schoonheden* (Dutch). They had no idea that its success would be worldwide, with translations into German, French, and English (*The Fate of the Sleeping Beauties*).

Upon completing the book about the Dovaz collection, Ard and Arnoud received more and more tips about barns in France, Portugal, England, Switzerland, Austria, and Italy, where so-called sleeping beauties were languishing. They often travelled together to take a look at these hidden treasures, and photographed or filmed them for posterity.

Next, they wrote a book about *Bijzondere autokerkhoven* (Dutch) published in November

Ard op de Weegh in a Bugatti T57C Stelvio. (Photo collection Op de Weegh)

Arnoud op de Weegh in a 1916 Oldsmobile Model 44 Speedster; he is not hiding the fact that he adores pre-war vehicles. (Photo collection Op de Weegh)

2011, in which they described several of the oldest remaining automobile graveyards.

The third book (*Bijzondere mensen, autocollecties, verhalen*) (Dutch) appeared in June 2013, and described nine persons who have made significant contributions to the maintenance of classic automobiles in the Netherlands and Belgium.

Since 2012 both authors have been writing regularly for several Duch and international magazines about classic automobiles.

Many of their activities may be followed on their website: www.extraordinarycarcollections.com.

Acknowledgements

Without the incredible support of numerous lovers of classic automobiles, crazy fans, specialists of particular car makes, owners, and people on internet forums, this book would never have come into being.

Many of these persons provided pieces of the puzzle; some even worked actively with us, trying to put the pieces in the right places. At times, we lost sight of the whole because of the very large number of contacts we had. Therefore, we apologise to those we may have inadvertently omitted in the list that follows:

The Jansen family (Jancia.eu), Jaap Braam Ruben, Bruno Vendiesse, Noek Stevens (Classic Skills), Kees Jansen, Gerard Lansink, Christian Huet, André Dufilho, Lionel Patenostre, John Barton, Peter Mullin, Richard Adatto, Kay Hottendorff, Jeroen Vossen, Marc Kohler, Heinz W Jordan, Bernhard Graf-Saner, David Gulick, Adrian van der Kroft, Piet Janssen, Signe Schlumpf, Charles Kengen, Hans Sneep, Bart Oosterling, Dick Ploeg, Karel Nestrojil, Peter Zinck, Christoph Seiler (Museum Autovision), Martin Meyer, Martien van Rietschoten, Kevin Wheatcroft, Nico and Nick Aaldering, Lionel Decrey, Dick Ploeg, Christoph Seiler (Autovision).

In addition to these and other helpful people, there were of course also those who constantly ignored us and even deliberately obstructed our efforts. Obviously we will not mention any names. Nevertheless, we are grateful to them as well because their attitude over and over again prompted us to persevere, and encouraged us to complete the project.

Finally, we wish to thank our partners, Louise and Jill, for their enormous support and patience throughout.

A T46 chassis from the museum's reserve collection; ready to be rebuilt.
(Photo collection Jean Marc Kohler)

Opposite: The characteristic lamp posts that grace the museum and that Fritz Schlumpf had fashioned after the lamp posts on a Parisian bridge (Alexander III bridge). (Photo collection Op de Weegh)

1937 Peugeot Darl'Mat in the Malmerspach collection. (Photo collection Op de Weegh)

List of the collection

List of the Mulhouse museum collection

On the next pages you will see a list of all vehicles that were in the Schlumpf museum (Mulhouse) when the workers occupied it in March 1977. We also include Fritz and Hans Schlumpf's museum reserve collection. To give a good idea of the prices Fritz and Hans paid for these vehicles, we provide the dates of purchase and the amounts. Moreover, in the last columns you will see the various appraisal values according to Christie's and Christian Huet (hired by Fritz Schlumpf) and Poulain and Chappelon (on behalf of the French government).

We have made the list as complete as possible on the basis of documentation at our disposal, and therefore assume that it is correct. Yet, we cannot guarantee this. Modifications reserved.

1902 Serpollet Paris-Madrid. (Photo collection Op de Weegh)

REF #	Marque	Type	Year	Chassis #	Engine #	Purchased	Bought for	Currency	Purchased from	Hervé Poulain (F)	Chappelon (F)	Huet (F)	Christie's (F)
3	Bugatti	Hermes-Mathis	1905	30		6/12/1964	36,000	F	Pozzoli	200,000	220,000	1,000,000	1,300,000
5	Bugatti	16	1912	715	715	4/11/1963	60,000	F	Bugatti	300,000	290,000	1,400,000	1,800,000
10	Bugatti	19				4/11/1963	2,000	F	Bugatti	75,000	50,000	650,000	700,000
15	Bugatti	T13	1911	484	130	1/26/1966	7,000	FS	Herplac	50,000	40,000	400,000	310,000
16	Bugatti	T13				1/6/1966	40,000	F	Pozzoli	90,000	60,000	400,000	390,000
17	Bugatti	T13	1920	765	470	3/1/1964	3,000	Dollar	Shakespeare	110,000	70,000	400,000	500,000
20	Bugatti	T22A		2253		4/26/1966	500	Dollar	Tuzex	15,000	20,000	150,000	220,000
25	Bugatti	T23	1921	2385	787	3/21/1963	11,000	F	Barré	40,000	20,000	400,000	250,000
26	Bugatti	T23	1913	531	181	5/23/1963	300	Pound	Idee	75,000	35,000	400,000	450,000
27	Bugatti	T23	1921	995		8/29/1962	8,000	F	Binda	70,000	25,000	330,000	260,000
30	Bugatti	T28	1921	5001	5001	4/11/1963	20,000	F	Bugatti	250,000	120,000	900,000	1,100,000
31	Bugatti	T30A	1926	4727	571	7/31/1961	1,900	F	Sipp	40,000	30,000	550,000	160,000
34	Bugatti	T32	1923	321461	1461	4/11/1963	20,000	F	Bugatti	300,000	40,000	2,000,000	2,000,000
35	Bugatti	T35	1925	4492	38	12/17/1963	1,400	Dollar	Fields	130,000	40,000	900,000	850,000
36	Bugatti	T35	1925	4565	13A	2/5/1964	70,000	Pes	Vina	150,000	50,000	900,000	900,000
37	Bugatti	T35A	1925	4612	42	4/23/1963	4,000	F	Eckert	130,000	50,000	600,000	550,000
38	Bugatti	T35B	1925	4611	104	9/28/1962	3,500	F	Eckert	160,000	50,000	1,100,000	1,120,000
39	Bugatti	T35	1929	4934	182	7/12/1963	7,000	F	Sergent van Giesen	170,000	55,000	900,000	1,000,000
40	Bugatti	T35				3/1/1964	3,000	Dollar	Shakespeare	130,000	60,000	900,000	0
41	Bugatti	T35A	1926	4753	83A	8/28/1962	10,000	F	Binda	130,000	40,000	600,000	550,000
42	Bugatti	T35TC	1928	4868	132T	11/17/1964	7,000	F	Eckert	150,000	30,000	1,900,000	1,850,000
43	Bugatti	T37	1928	4872	163	9/13/1963	1,700	Dollar	Vintage	200,000	30,000	1,900,000	1,700,000
44	Bugatti	T35B	1929	4923	191	2/3/1962	11,000	F	Libert	220,000	60,000	1,100,000	1,350,000
45	Bugatti	T35B	1929	4933	198TC	1/1/1939	5,000	F	Personal car	350,000	240,000	1,900,000	2,000,000
46	Bugatti	T51	1934	51151	109T	10/29/1964	8,000	FS	Eckert	200,000	70,000	1,000,000	1,100,000
55	Bugatti	T37	1926	37196	96	7/31/1961	2,100	F	Sac	120,000	38,000	480,000	525,000
56	Bugatti	T37	1928	37314	211C	7/29/1963	1,000	Dollar	Loucks	100,000	40,000	480,000	525,000
57	Bugatti	T37A	1929	37373	284	7/30/1962	5,500	F	Seyfried	150,000	45,000	550,000	660,000
65	Bugatti	T38	1927	38292	160	7/31/1964	1,600	F	Sraw	70,000	35,000	480,000	400,000
66	Bugatti	T38	1927	38404	259	11/17/1964	5,000	FS	Eckert	110,000	60,000	480,000	400,000
70	Bugatti	T40A	1929	40230	120	7/31/1961	2,400	F	Sipp	90,000	60,000	350,000	340,000
73	Bugatti	T40	1927	40524		3/21/1964	5,000	F	Barré	65,000	40,000	250,000	370,000
74	Bugatti	T40		40534		12/10/1962	7,500	F	Garino	30,000	30,000	250,000	300,000
75	Bugatti	T40	1928	40673		8/28/1962	7,000	F	Binda	80,000	80,000	330,000	420,000
76	Bugatti	T40	1930	40684		3/1/1964	2,500	Dollar	Shakespeare	120,000	95,000	600,000	550,000
78	Bugatti	T40		40747		10/5/1962	2,000	F	Mette	20,000	20,000	150,000	220,000
79	Bugatti	T40	1929	40811	157	4/11/1963	20,000	F	Bugatti	70,000	30,000	350,000	375,000
90	Bugatti	T41	1926	41100	41100	4/11/1963	2,500	Dollar	Bugatti	3,500,000	3,500,000	30,000,000	28,500,000
91	Bugatti	T41	1933	41131	41131	3/1/1964	8,500	Dollar	Shakespeare	2,500,000	3,200,000	15,000,000	17,000,000
92	Bugatti	T41					150,000	Dollar		600,000	1,750,000	5,000,000	8,000,000
100	Bugatti	T43	1927	43173	14	1/14/1963	2,500	FS	Suter	110,000	100,000	700,000	600,000
101	Bugatti	T43	1930	43206	54	10/20/1964	28,000	F	Barré	250,000	110,000	900,000	780,000
102	Bugatti	T43	1928	43213	53	12/10/1964	20,000	f	Mortarini	170,000	100,000	900,000	780,000
103	Bugatti	T43	1928	43226	61	8/8/1963	1,000	F	Hogg	160,000	85,000	800,000	700,000
104	Bugatti	T43	1928	43227	110	3/28/1963	4,000	FS	Eckert	170,000	100,000	850,000	720,000
105	Bugatti	T43	1929	43276	156	7/11/1963	1,700	Dollar	Feinstein	150,000	50,000	800,000	780,000
106	Bugatti	T43	1931	43298	140	7/31/1961	2,150	F	Sac	230,000	110,000	800,000	700,000
107	Bugatti	T43	1929	43258	89	4/19/1963	4,000	FS	Eckert	250,000	110,000	900,000	700,000
108	Bugatti	T44				4/19/1963	4,000	FS	Eckert	80,000	60,000	0	0
110	Bugatti	T44	1929	441205	934		Unknown			0	0	600,000	560,000
116	Bugatti	T44				4/17/1963	Unknown		Barré	130,000	100,000	0	0
118	Bugatti	T44	1926	44664	304	6/4/1964	8,000	F	Dayoé	40,000	25,000	200,000	200,000
125	Bugatti	T45	1929	47156		4/11/1963	25,000	F	Bugatti	500,000	150,000	2,500,000	2,750,000
130	Bugatti	T46	1932	46574	197S	7/5/1963	5,865	F	Korin	130,000	100,000	600,000	610,000
131	Bugatti	T46	1931	46479	310	4/11/1963	3,000	F	Bugatti	50,000	50,000	650,000	880,000
132	Bugatti	T46	1930	46434	294	4/11/1963	3,000	F	Bugatti	40,000	50,000	600,000	880,000
133	Bugatti	T46	1929	46125	5	3/1/1964	2,500	Dollar	Shakespeare	70,000	70,000	500,000	720,000
134	Bugatti	T46	1930	46188	78	4/11/1963	5,000	F	Bugatti	90,000	130,000	450,000	500,000
135	Bugatti	T46S	1930	46287	100S	3/1/1964	2,500	Dollar	Shakespeare	50,000	40,000	600,000	530,000
136	Bugatti	T46	1931	46482	327	7/23/1963	1,400	Dollar	Rhéault	350,000	500,000	2,500,000	1,950,000
137	Bugatti	T46	1931	46523	394	3/1/1964	2,500	Dollar	Shakespeare	150,000	90,000	900,000	790,000
138	Bugatti	T46	1931	46552	449	4/11/1963	5,000	F	Bugatti	55,000	45,000	350,000	250,000
139	Bugatti	T46	1931	46555	414	8/28/1962	5,000	F	Sac	70,000	50,000	600,000	480,000
140	Bugatti	T46S	1932	46560	1S	7/24/1961	50,000	F	Sipp	90,000	120,000	1,000,000	1,700,000
141	Bugatti	T46	1930	46325	295	11/26/1963	6,500	F	Raffaelli	60,000	50,000	450,000	420,000
149	Bugatti	T47	1930	47155		4/11/1963	25,000	F	Bugatti	450,000	120,000	2,500,000	2,750,000
150	Bugatti	T49	1931	49172	77	10/19/1964	6,000	FS	Eckert	110,000	75,000	600,000	520,000
151	Bugatti	T49	1932	49210		3/19/1965	6,000	FS	Eckert	95,000	75,000	600,000	480,000
152	Bugatti	T49	1931	49236		4/13/1964	5,000	F	André	50,000	45,000	300,000	290,000
153	Bugatti	T49	1932	49135	L178	1/26/1965	5,500	FS	Eckert	70,000	65,000	400,000	420,000
154	Bugatti	T49	1933	49368		4/22/1964	3,000	F	Didiot	45,000	30,000	300,000	330,000
155	Bugatti	T49	1933	49414		8/17/1961	2,000	F	Goux	90,000	70,000	450,000	430,000
156	Bugatti	T49	1932	49445	L342	4/19/1963	3,000	FS	Eckert	100,000	70,000	550,000	500,000
157	Bugatti	T49	1934	49471		2/2/1964	1,000	F	Granoff	100,000	60,000	550,000	465,000
158	Bugatti	T49	1934	49501	L399	7/17/1963	1,400	Dollar	Bolton	90,000	70,000	600,000	525,000
159	Bugatti	T49	1934	49559		8/16/1963	4,000	F	Neuilly Sport	110,000	80,000	400,000	500,000
160	Bugatti	T49	1934	49564	L450	12/10/1964	13,000	F	Renfer	95,000	65,000	500,000	410,000
161	Bugatti	T49		49476		8/24/1964	5,000	FS	Dursteler	90,000	70,000	500,000	450,000
162	Bugatti	T49		49218		3/1/1964	2,500	Dollar	Shakespeare	70,000	35,000	500,000	375,000
170	Bugatti	T50	1931	50130		3/1/1964	2,500	Dollar	Shakespeare	100,000	65,000	600,000	600,000

REF #	Marque	Type	Year	Chassis #	Engine #	Purchased	Bought for	Currency	Purchased from	Hervé Poulain (F)	Chappelon (F)	Huet (F)	Christie's (F)
171	Bugatti	T50	1933	50160	20T	3/1/1964	2,500	Dollar	Shakespeare	150,000	50,000	850,000	940,000
172	Bugatti	T59/50B		50180		1/6/1966	54,600	F	Pozzoli	300,000	450,000	4,500,000	4,200,000
173	Bugatti	T50B	1936	50180	50B1	4/11/1963	100,000	F	Bugatti	600,000	650,000	5,000,000	5,100,000
180	Bugatti	T51	1931	51124	5	4/19/1963	4,000	F	Eckert	300,000	120,000	1,500,000	1,750,000
181	Bugatti	T51A	1931	51142	13	9/9/1964	2,100	Dollar	Bechelly	350,000	100,000	1,600,000	1,850,000
182	Bugatti	T51A	1932	51134A		9/17/1964	1,625	Dollar	Vintage	100,000	35,000	2,300,000	2,200,000
183	Bugatti	T51		51712		10/29/1964	Unknown		Eckert	10,000	0	1,200,000	900,000
190	Bugatti	T52				12/14/1963	2,700	F	Klein	0	0	0	0
191	Bugatti	T52		409A	81745	9/6/1963	24,000	PES	Vina	25,000	25,000	80,000	94,000
192	Bugatti	T52		221A	54038	9/6/1963	18,000	PES	Vina	25,000	25,000	80,000	94,000
193	Bugatti	T52				1/1/1952	200	F	Christen	25,000	0	80,000	94,000
199	Bugatti	T53	1931	53002		4/11/1963	3,000	F	Bugatti	30,000	0	1,500,000	1,300,000
200	Bugatti	T55	1932	55224	2ACT	8/26/1963	400	Pound	Gillingham	160,000	40,000	1,200,000	1,500,000
201	Bugatti	T55	1931	55203	3	3/1/1964	2,500	Dollar	Shakespeare	180,000	85,000	1,200,000	1,450,000
202	Bugatti	T55	1931	55204		2/5/1964	25,000	F	Bouyer	250,000	140,000	1,700,000	1,550,000
203	Bugatti	T55	1932	55212	22	4/19/1963	4,000	FS	Eckert	250,000	130,000	1,700,000	1,550,000
204	Bugatti	T55	1932	55215	19	3/1/1964	3,000	Dollar	Shakespeare	280,000	155,000	1,900,000	1,800,000
205	Bugatti	T55	1933	55225	23	6/24/1963	650	Pound	Gillingham	180,000	130,000	1,600,000	1,550,000
206	Bugatti	T55	1932	55237	37	3/1/1964	3,000	Dollar	Shakespeare	280,000	120,000	1,900,000	1,800,000
207	Bugatti	T55	1933	55218	600 (Ex T44)	8/24/1964	5,000	FS	Dursteler	80,000	20,000	1,100,000	1,050,000
215	Bugatti	T56	1931	56S-1001		3/1/1964	2,000	Dollar	Shakespeare	40,000	50,000	500,000	450,000
225	Bugatti	T57	1936	57341	241	7/31/1961	2,000	F	Sac	60,000	50,000	350,000	260,000
226	Bugatti	T57	1935	57356	247	8/28/1962	6,000	F	Binda	140,000	65,000	400,000	385,000
227	Bugatti	T57	1935	57265	213	3/1/1964	2,500	Dollar	Shakespeare	0	0	450,000	245,000
228	Bugatti	T57	1936	57386	281	8/28/1962	1,200	F	Sipp	50,000	55,000	300,000	230,000
229	Bugatti	T57				12/10/1962	2,250	F	Schwend	65,000	45,000	350,000	0
230	Bugatti	T57	1936	57403	296	3/18/1962	5,750	F	Novo	110,000	45,000	450,000	420,000
231	Bugatti	T57	1936	57417	292	3/1/1964	2,500	Dollar	Shakespeare	100,000	50,000	600,000	550,000
232	Bugatti	T57	1936	57457	343	8/28/1962	2,400	F	Sipp	120,000	50,000	550,000	615,000
233	Bugatti	T57C	1937	57496	11C	6/15/1963	3,000	FS	Orange	130,000	85,000	450,000	410,000
237	Bugatti	T57	1938	57611	497	1/23/1963	5,000	F	Planche	100,000	100,000	400,000	400,000
238	Bugatti	T57	1936	57464	241	3/1/1964	2,500	Dollar	Shakespeare	10,000	10,000	300,000	100,000
239	Bugatti	T57	1939	57721		8/16/1963	9,500	F	Neuilly Sport	100,000	100,000	450,000	425,000
240	Bugatti	T57	1939	57764		3/1/1964	2,500	Dollar	Shakespeare	60,000	60,000	700,000	680,000
241	Bugatti	T57	1938	57616	21C	4/17/1963	12,000	F	Barré	130,000	100,000	250,000	385,000
242	Bugatti	T57				9/9/1961	1,500	F	Trivier	20,000	0	0	0
250	Bugatti	T57C	1938	57539/57663	396	5/15/1963	6,000	FS	Orange	190,000	140,000	800,000	825,000
252	Bugatti	T57C	1938	57636	C22	7/24/1961	30,000	F	Sipp	150,000	140,000	450,000	640,000
253	Bugatti	T57C				3/1/1964	3,000	Dollar	Shakespeare	60,000	0	0	0
254	Bugatti	T57C	1938	57747	60C	8/7/1961	8,000	F	Sipp	180,000	150,000	800,000	880,000
255	Bugatti	T57C	1939	57789	80C	3/1/1964	3,000	Dollar	Shakespeare	160,000	150,000	550,000	670,000
260	Bugatti	T57S	1936	57471	11S	1/31/1961	1,000	Dollar	Bond	250,000	150,000	1,800,000	1,650,000
261	Bugatti	T57S	1936	57481	S1003	3/1/1964	3,000	Dollar	Shakespeare	250,000	150,000	1,800,000	1,320,000
262	Bugatti	T57S	1937	57543	31S	3/1/1964	3,000	Dollar	Shakespeare	260,000	200,000	1,800,000	1,750,000
263	Bugatti	T57S	1937	57572	38S	2/18/1964	700	Pound	Lord O'Neil	300,000	100,000	1,800,000	1,700,000
268	Bugatti	T57S	1938	57618		10/31/1963	6,500	F	Mette	20,000	25,000	1,200,000	1,100,000
269	Bugatti	T57SC	1937	57451	7S	4/22/1969	60,000	F	Anselin	260,000	300,000	1,900,000	2,000,000
270	Bugatti	T57SC	1936	57441	329	9/7/1962	4,000	FS	Renaud	260,000	350,000	1,900,000	2,000,000
271	Bugatti	T57SC	1937	57561	S1004	3/1/1964	3,000	Dollar	Shakespeare	150,000	50,000	1,200,000	1,800,000
272	Bugatti	T57S	1937	57571	34S	8/12/1963	1,700	Dollar	Shakespeare	290,000	120,000	1,800,000	1,750,000
273	Bugatti	T57SC	1938	57602	43S	7/18/1963	550	Pound	Pryor	300,000	120,000	1,900,000	1,950,000
285	Bugatti	T64	1935	57333	234	4/11/1963	30,000	F	Bugatti	270,000	150,000	2,500,000	2,200,000
286	Bugatti	T68	1942			4/11/1963	1,000	F	Bugatti	40,000	50,000	450,000	375,000
287	Bugatti	T73	1948	73C003		4/11/1963	5,000	F	Bugatti	50,000	25,000	350,000	550,000
288	Bugatti	T73	1947	73001	73A	4/11/1963	1,000	F	Bugatti	20,000	15,000	500,000	975,000
290	Bugatti	T101	1951	101500		6/20/1961	8,000	F	Seyfried	120,000	70,000	900,000	880,000
291	Bugatti	T101	1951	101503	101504	4/11/1963	20,000	F	Bugatti	100,000	100,000	800,000	920,000
292	Bugatti	T101C	1951	57454	101503	4/11/1963	20,000	F	Bugatti	100,000	100,000	900,000	1,900,000
295	Bugatti	T101		101403		7/31/1964	15,000	F	Bugatti	40,000	35,000	800,000	880,000
296	Bugatti	T251	1956	251001	1	4/11/1963	50,000	F	Bugatti	300,000	110,000	2,500,000	2,200,000
297	Bugatti	T251	1956	251002	13	4/11/1963	50,000	F	Bugatti	300,000	130,000	2,500,000	2,200,000
298	Bugatti	T252	1957	252299		4/11/1963	10,000	F	Bugatti	80,000	60,000	1,300,000	950,000
299	Bugatti	T252	1957	288		4/11/1963	10,000	F	Bugatti	90,000	80,000	800,000	80,000
1000	A.B.C.	918	1921		5198 S1 H	1/6/1966	900	F	Pozzoli	6,000	4,000	15,000	36,000
1020	Alfa Romeo	6C1750	1931	10814365	10814365	11/5/1962	3,000	FS	Minoretti	150,000	150,000	600,000	660,000
1022	Alfa Romeo	6C1750	1937	10814342		10/30/1962	1,000	FS	Tognazzo	30,000	25,000	100,000	100,000
1030	Alfa Romeo	8C2300	1932	2211069	2211069	1/9/1963	1,500	FS	Eckert	180,000	170,000	650,000	880,000
1050	Alfa Romeo	8C2300				8/28/1962	400	Pound	Lord O'Neil	200,000	160,000	400,000	950,000
1055	Alfa Romeo	412		412038	412152	9/28/1962	1,200	FS	Eckert	140,000	0	1,200,000	1,550,000
1065	Alfa Romeo	8C2900		422039		11/5/1962	4,000	FS	Eckert	140,000	80,000	1,000,000	1,000,000
1066	Alfa Romeo	8C2900		412034	422026	1/9/1963	4,500	FS	Eckert	140,000	80,000	1,000,000	1,000,000
1067	Alfa Romeo	8C2900B	1936	412004	422004	3/29/1963	6,000	FS	Eckert	120,000	80,000	800,000	0
1068	Alfa Romeo					4/19/1963	8,000	FS	Eckert	22,000	0	0	0
1070	Alfa Romeo	C52 1900	1952	AR1359	1309302	4/3/1963	6,000	FS	Eckert	110,000	65,000	1,700,000	1,200,000
1099	Altos					11/19/1962	1,500	F	Grison	2,000	0	0	0
1100	Amilcar	CGSS	1925			12/27/1963	850	F	Sennes	26,000	25,000	100,000	132,000
1102	Amilcar	CGSS	1926		1004	7/31/1961	1,000	F	Sipp	25,000	20,000	80,000	132,000
1105	Amilcar	C6	1926	11028	90020	12/10/1963	3,000	F	Riehl	130,000	35,000	400,000	420,000
1120	Audi	15/50 PS	1924	3651	3682	5/31/1967	15,000	DM	Intrac	40,000	20,000	90,000	190,000
1125	Austin	Seven				9/6/1963	18,000	PES	Vina	1,000	0	0	0

REF #	Marque	Type	Year	Chassis #	Engine #	Purchased	Bought for	Currency	Purchased from	Hervé Poulain (F)	Chappelon (F)	Huet (F)	Christie's (F)
1133	Austro Daimler	3 Litres	1929	11921	24003	6/12/1963	4,650	F	Pfluger	60,000	25,000	50,000	260,000
1160	Ballot	3 Litres	1921	3	1008	4/10/1964	90,000	PES	Vina	300,000	200,000	900,000	1,800,000
1162	Ballot	RH3	1929	6572	65487	9/23/1964	8,000	FS	Filipinetti	65,000	30,000	150,000	140,000
1164	Ballot	2LTS	1925	3570	47600	11/21/1962	1,200	F	Spaenlin	20,000	10,000	150,000	105,000
1170	Barré		1897	5562		8/24/1964	10,000	FS	Dursteler	20,000	20,000	120,000	182,000
1172	Barré	4FM	1912	8369	8369	9/25/1962	9,000	F	Vincent	45,000	30,000	70,000	110,000
1180	Baudier	3HP	1900	1082	13237	11/19/1962	7,500	F	Grison	20,000	15,000	50,000	150,000
1200	Bentley	4,5 Litre	1937	B39GY	Z9BL	3/27/1963	525	Pound	Mitchell	25,000	45,000	100,000	232,000
1204	Bentley	8 Litre	1931	YM 5030	BM 7190	9/23/1964	25,000	FS	Filipinetti	170,000	100,000	500,000	540,000
1208	Bentley	MK VI	1950	B 557 FU	B 529 F	8/28/1962	2,500	F	Sipp	30,000	35,000	50,000	93,000
1212	Bentley	MK VI	1948	B 284 CF	DB 1420	10/30/1963	5,000	FS	Clavel	75,000	75,000	300,000	225,000
1230	Benz	Victoria	1893		55	5/8/1962	Uknown		Delecroix	120,000	100,000	700,000	700,000
1240	Benz	Vélo	1897	203-1190 K	48-2020	1/4/1966	52,500	F	Renfer	80,000	60,000	400,000	330,000
1242	Benz	Vélo	1898			8/25/1962	21,800	F	Coffre	80,000	55,000	250,000	190,000
1243	Benz	Vélo	1898	20		7/3/1970	13,000	F	Renel	40,000	10,000	250,000	190,000
1244	Benz	Ideal	1901	1334	1300	8/24/1964	10,000	FS	Dursteler	90,000	80,000	400,000	385,000
1245	Benz	Vélo	1896	203	48-2020	6/5/1968	30,000	DM	Eckert	65,000	50,000	430,000	400,000
1260	Benz	Comfortable				8/3/1966	1,830	Pound	Loxham	70,000	60,000	480,000	350,000
1280	Benz					3/29/1965	35,000	F	Criqui	75,000	55,000	0	0
1300	BNC	XIIC	1928	21056	21036	8/28/1962	3,000	F	Sac	35,000	30,000	120,000	135,000
1310	Leon Bollée		1896	812		10/31/1962	20,000	F	Mette	18,000	15,000	60,000	245,000
1320	Brasier	VL	1910	820M	850 M	8/27/1962	10,500	F	Thuysbaert	25,000	25,000	100,000	105,000
1326	Brasier	KD	1906	KD 38	30	4/20/1964	15,000	F	Larroude	110,000	70,000	250,000	235,000
1340	Charron	XIIC	1910	173	14320	1/23/1962	3,000	F	Letort	30,000	20,000	80,000	82,000
1350	Cisitalia	D46	1946/48	26	27	7/22/1963	5,000	FS	Eckert	40,000	25,000	130,000	300,000
1375	Citroën	5CV	1922	1132	VA21	8/27/1962	500	F	Doumerc	3,000	5,000	20,000	28,000
1376	Citroën	5CV				4/7/1964	800	F	Mallebay	4,000	4,000	10,000	8,000
1377	Citroën	5CV	1923		9615	8/8/1961	350	F	Lepage	7,000	10,000	20,000	28,000
1378	Citroën	5CV	1923	9331	VA 3153	8/10/1961	250	F	Thouvenin	7,000	0	20,000	28,000
1379	Citroën	5CV			29373	5/31/1961	1,500	F	Merklen	10,000	7,000	25,000	30,000
1410	Clément Bayard	4M3	1911	18706	18737	3/21/1963	4,000	F	Barré	15,000	10,000	90,000	80,000
1412	Clément Bayard	CB1	1912		19516	9/25/1962	9,000	F	Vincent	40,000	30,000	90,000	110,000
1414	Clément Bayard	LM4	1913	23295		3/21/1963	2,000	F	Barré	4,000	2,500	90,000	33,000
1420	Clément Bayard	Gladiator	1900		15717	8/28/1962	15,000	F	Binda	25,000	20,000	80,000	195,000
1425	Clément Bayard	VCP	1900		469	9/15/1964	8,000	FS	Filipinetti	40,000	30,000	120,000	200,000
1450	Daimler	Bus	1899			8/11/1966	5,000	Pound	Loxham	100,000	60,000	40,000	255,000
1460	Daimler	38HP	1912			9/23/1964	42,500	FS	Filipinetti	130,000	60,000	180,000	225,000
1470	Daimler	V26	1934	38282	22500	3/23/1963	200	Pound	Bennet	20,000	17,000	80,000	78,000
1480	Daimler	32 HP	1938	44268	26705	3/12/1963	100	Pound	Adams	15,000	14,000	80,000	90,000
1490	Daimler	DB18	1949	53175	28564	3/18/1963	125	Pound	Crockford	15,000	16,000	90,000	53,000
1500	Daimler	DF 302	1954	82025	48554	3/18/1963	570	Pound	French	30,000	20,000	50,000	77,000
1564	Darracq	C	1901			9/25/1962	16,000	F	Vincent	60,000	35,000	120,000	165,000
1565	Darracq	L	1903			11/7/1962	12,000	F	Letort	30,000	35,000	80,000	160,000
1566	Darracq	P	1910		5536	9/18/1962	4,000	F	Malartre	5,000	3,500	20,000	33,000
1567	Darracq		1910		814F	11/14/1962	6,500	F	Ruyer	20,000	30,000	60,000	99,000
1568	Darracq	20/28 HP	1907	16042	12870	9/25/1964	20,000	F	Dax Auto	90,000	90,000	300,000	250,000
1570	Decauville	10 HP	1903	3500		6/18/1957	1,500	F	Hartzer	70,000	30,000	120,000	121,000
1590	De Dion Bouton	L	1902	37	8218	9/12/1964	20,000	F	Kerloch	65,000	35,000	80,000	138,000
1591	De Dion Bouton	EA	1901	331	1840	8/1/1964	20,000	F	Rabufetti	40,000	35,000	70,000	125,000
1592	De Dion Bouton	G	1901	510	5508	10/10/1962	15,000	F	Sac	40,000	35,000	70,000	125,000
1593	De Dion Bouton	G	1901	570	4539	11/9/1962	5,000	F	Djaniguian	40,000	35,000	70,000	125,000
1594	De Dion Bouton		1901	666	4536	12/7/1962	9,000	F	Honoré	40,000	35,000	70,000	125,000
1595	De Dion Bouton	G	1901	868	4670		9,500	F	Mette	40,000	35,000	70,000	125,000
1596	De Dion Bouton	G	1901	1133	5741	8/12/1966	18,000	F	Broussine	40,000	35,000	70,000	125,000
1597	De Dion Bouton		1901	1195	5980	1/29/1965	16,000	F	Dobson	45,000	35,000	90,000	125,000
1598	De Dion Bouton	G	1901	1430	6109	1/23/1962	6,650	F	Joker	60,000	35,000	80,000	130,000
1601	De Dion Bouton						Uknown		Filipinetti	5,000	5,000	20,000	47,000
1602	De Dion Bouton					9/25/1962	4,000	F	Thuysbaert	7,000	3,000	20,000	47,000
1603	De Dion Bouton					12/4/1964	6,000	F	Demoto	8,000	6,000	15,000	22,000
1614	De Dion Bouton	H	1902		14181	8/24/1964	10,000	FS	Dursteler	30,000	25,000	80,000	120,000

REF #	Marque	Type	Year	Chassis #	Engine #	Purchased	Bought for	Currency	Purchased from	Hervé Poulain (F)	Chappelon (F)	Huet (F)	Christie's (F)
1615	De Dion Bouton	AL	1906	520	273	8/24/1964	10,000	FS	Dursteler	70,000	35,000	100,000	95,000
1616	De Dion Bouton	J	1902	164	10347	3/18/1963	15,000	F	Lyon	30,000	20,000	80,000	102,000
1617	De Dion Bouton	V	1904	412	14968	8/27/1962	13,500	F	Thuysbaert	40,000	30,000	90,000	100,000
1618	De Dion Bouton	V	1903		14892	9/18/1962	9,000	F	Malartre	35,000	25,000	80,000	105,000
1620	De Dion Bouton	8CV	1901		488	9/7/1962	17,500	F	Djaniguian	45,000	30,000	110,000	127,000
1625	De Dion Bouton	AO	1906	55		10/10/1962	6,000	F	Sac	25,000	15,000	110,000	115,000
1626	De Dion Bouton	BG			22924	9/27/1962	3,000	F	Cibié	60,000	30,000	80,000	120,000
1627	De Dion Bouton	BO2	1909		25309	9/27/1962	3,500	F	Cibié	10,000	10,000	40,000	66,000
1630	De Dion Bouton		1904		718	2/8/1963	20,000	F	Pasco	50,000	40,000	110,000	127,000
1631	De Dion Bouton	S	1907		1942B	9/18/1962	14,000	F	Malartre	40,000	30,000	120,000	121,000
1635	De Dion Bouton	EA	1913		17437	9/18/1962	11,000	F	Malartre	50,000	35,000	120,000	110,000
1636	De Dion Bouton	12CV	1912		13030	10/31/1962	3,200	FS	Hüni	30,000	18,000	90,000	100,000
1637	De Dion Bouton	CL	1910	197	4803	3/21/1963	4,000	F	Barré	25,000	20,000	80,000	92,000
1638	De Dion Bouton	DH	1912		87	8/28/1962	20,000	F	Sipp	30,000	20,000	90,000	0
1639	De Dion Bouton	DX	1913	623	12413	8/27/1962	8,000	F	Thuysbaert	25,000	10,000	0	90,000
1650	De Dion Bouton		1912	620	9503	11/7/1962	7,500	F	Raffaelli	45,000	30,000	80,000	110,000
1655	De Dion Bouton	12/14CB	1914		7386C	4/24/1964	7,000	F	Lacroix	90,000	45,000	200,000	140,000
1680	Delage	F	1905	663	24,181	7/31/1961	1,800	F	Sipp	30,000	30,000	80,000	127,000
1682	Delage	F	1908	502	22906	7/31/1961	2,000	F	Sipp	70,000	35,000	250,000	500,000
1710	Delahaye	28A	1908	2175	78	2/3/1962	8,000	F	Libert	35,000	25,000	90,000	88,000
1714	Delahaye		1909		3674	11/2/1962	15,000	F	Gazériot	110,000	45,000	230,000	200,000
1716	Delahaye	87	1912	21804	VS1716	3/21/1963	4,000	F	Barré	0	5,500	0	0
1720	Delahaye	32	1914		8938	1/23/1962	6,000	F	Letort	70,000	45,000	170,000	260,000
1730	Delauney-Belleville	F6	1912	2196	1595Y	9/11/1963	6,000	F	Villa	90,000	70,000	180,000	245,000
1736	Delauney-Belleville	H6B	1913	5523Y		9/11/1962	7,000	F	Malartre	75,000	50,000	160,000	210,000
1740	Dufaux	Gordon Bennet	1904	AD13	AD3	3/17/1964	10,000	FS	Tonpasse	300,000	175,000	1,200,000	1,900,000
1744	Dufaux					1/6/1966	750	FS	Mercplac	500	0	30,000	0
1750	Esculape		1900	48		11/19/1962	5,500	FS	Grison	15,000	10,000	70,000	132,000
1760	Farman	A6	1921		55	9/10/1962	15,000	F	Malartre	160,000	180,000	450,000	525,000
1762	Farman	A6B	1927	610	610	1/13/1966	22,500	F	Pozzoli	120,000	150,000	400,000	400,000
1772	Ferrari	166	1948	0001F	2	6/18/1963	4,000	FS	Eckert	150,000	50,000	650,000	715,000
1775	Ferrari	500	1952	0512MD	0512MD	6/18/1963	5,000	FS	Eckert	180,000	75,000	500,000	550,000
1780	Ferrari	125	1950			10/23/1963	801,600	Lit	Girard	150,000	95,000	650,000	770,000
1785	Ferrari	500	1952	184F2	184F2	10/23/1963	701,400	Lit	Girard	180,000	75,000	700,000	770,000
1790	Ferrari	250MM	1953	230MM	230MM	10/19/1964	6,000	FS	Eckert	130,000	65,000	700,000	525,000
1795	Ferrari	500TR	1957	0692MDTR	0692MDTR	9/24/1964	5,000	FS	Blancpain	130,000	95,000	450,000	500,000
1800	Ferrari	450AM	1954	450AM	493SA	5/1/1968	3,000	F	Bao Dai	50,000	50,000	350,000	450,000
1810	Ferrari	T158 F1	1963	5		3/26/1965	1,000,000	Lit	Ferrari	90,000	40,000	600,000	660,000
1811	Ferrari	512M				2/1/1973	5,000,000	Lit	Ferrari	200,000	150,000	0	0
1812	Ferrari	275				6/21/1971	26,100	FS	Filipinetti	150,000	120,000	0	0
1860	Fiat	509A	1925	109A 111138		8/28/1962	4,500	F	Binda	22,000	16,000	50,000	52,000
1862	Fiat	508S	1934	108CS/044028	508S/042.871	10/30/1962	1,500	F	Tognazzo	25,000	25,000	80,000	99,000
1890	Fouillaron	10HP	1902		7413	3/27/1962	15,500	F		55,000	35,000	70,000	137,000
1899	Gladiator	20HP	1907		3160	3/25/1962	3,200	F		20,000	30,000	110,000	105,000
1900	Gordini	T16	1952/54	35	49	6/15/1964	11,000	F	Gordini	160,000	90,000	650,000	610,000
1902	Gordini	T16	1952/54	34	33	6/15/1964	9,000	F	Gordini	150,000	85,000	650,000	610,000
1904	Gordini	T32	1955/56	41	54	6/15/1964	7,000	F	Gordini	200,000	120,000	700,000	720,000
1906	Gordini	T32	1955/56	42	47	6/15/1964	20,000	F	Gordini	200,000	140,000	700,000	720,000
1908	Gordini	17S	1953	39	53	6/15/1964	25,000	F	Gordini	90,000	45,000	300,000	275,000
1910	Gordini	20S	1952	18	42	6/15/1964	25,000	F	Gordini	100,000	65,000	350,000	310,000
1912	Gordini	20S	1954	43	40	6/15/1964	25,000	F	Gordini	120,000	70,000	350,000	310,000
1914	Gordini	23S	1953	19	58	6/15/1964	30,000	F	Gordini	150,000	80,000	350,000	375,000
1916	Gordini	26S		38S		10/14/1968	28,000	F	Brocart	50,000	90,000	400,000	610,000
1918	Gordini	15S	1953		44	6/15/1964	5,000	F	Gordini	100,000	80,000	700,000	500,000
1920	Gordini	24S	1957	37		6/15/1964	7,000	F	Gordini	140,000	0	700,000	500,000
1922	Gordini	Simca-8	1939	810404	810524	6/15/1964	4,000	F	Gordini	140,000	30,000	350,000	300,000
1924	Gordini	Simca-5	1937	1715	347-491	6/15/1964	7,000	F	Gordini	50,000	15,000	300,000	230,000
1926	Gordini	T15	1950			6/15/1964	Unknown		Gordini	65,000	35,000	300,000	330,000
2100	Gregoire	6/8HP	1910		393	7/31/1961	14,000	F	Scoupe	35,000	30,000	100,000	105,000

REF #	Marque	Type	Year	Chassis #	Engine #	Purchased	Bought for	Currency	Purchased from	Hervé Poulain (F)	Chappelon (F)	Huet (F)	Christie's (F)
2115	Guillemin-Le Gui	B2	1913	534	DEF2087	9/18/1962	8,000	F	Malartre	25,000	25,000	70,000	95,000
2120	Harley Davidson		1916			5/16/1963	195	Pound	Ellis	6,000	6,000	25,000	40,000
2122	Harley Davidson					5/16/1963	250	Pound	Ellis	10,000	6,000	25,000	20,000
2130	Hispano Suiza	Alfonse XIII	1912	1854	1854	1/6/1965	54,000	F	Pozzoli	60,000	100,000	350,000	465,000
2132	Hispano Suiza		1812	1851	1851	5/30/1963	11,000	F	Barré	25,000	35,000	150,000	225,000
2160	Hispano Suiza	H6B	1927	11856	301846	10/2/1963	5,000	F		220,000	160,000	300,000	550,000
2162	Hispano Suiza	H6C				3/18/1963	4,600	F	Sipp	80,000	60,000	250,000	320,000
2164	Hispano Suiza	K6	1935	15034	333073	7/31/1961	2,400	F	Sac	70,000	35,000	250,000	220,000
2166	Hispano Suiza	K6	1932	16027	333036	7/31/1961	2,600	F	Sac	100,000	90,000	300,000	200,000
2180	Hispano Suiza	J12	1933	14021	321057	10/12/1962	4,250	F	Loyens	260,000	175,000	550,000	825,000
2182	Hispano Suiza	J12	1934	13035	321121	1/6/1966	13,500	F	Pozzoli	250,000	200,000	550,000	1,350,000
2184	Hispano Suiza	J12	1934	14010	321036	4/26/1964	12,500	F	Kortarini	250,000	220,000	0	900,000
2220	Horch	450	1931	45268	45554	5/31/1967	10,000	DM	Intrac	60,000	25,000	500,000	385,000
2230	Horch	830	1935	83866	80866	7/31/1961	2,000	F	Sipp	25,000	15,000	350,000	230,000
2240	Horch	670	1932	67030	67039	4/19/1963	5,000	FS	Eckert	110,000	85,000	900,000	950,000
2250	Hurtu		1897	181	22	9/10/1962	6,000	F	Lotart	40,000	35,000	140,000	231,000
2250	Maserati	250F	1957	2511		7/1/1963	12,000	F	Eckert	250,000	110,000	1,200,000	1,375,000
2256	Hurtu	23K	1907		6073	10/18/1962	12,000	F	Meed	20,000	15,000	45,000	72,000
2260	Indian					4/30/1963	70	Pound	Ellis	1,500	3,000	5,000	4,000
2266	Indian		1945		228222	5/16/1963	95	Pound	Ellis	4,000	4,000	15,000	17,000
2310	Isotta Fraschini	8A	1926	680	675	3/6/1964	5,200	FS	Injurstrom	130,000	70,000	550,000	510,000
2314	Isotta Fraschini	8A	1926	1512	1574	3/16/1963	400	Pound	Killis	250,000	200,000	600,000	600,000
2320	Isotta Fraschini	8A	1926	640	634	10/8/1962	1,500	FS	Truninger	250,000	200,000	650,000	625,000
2330	Jacquot		1876			11/16/1961	30,000	F	Djaniguian	200,000	60,000	500,000	800,000
2340	S.S1	16 HP	1934/35	248108		10/19/1964	5,000	FS	Eckert	27,000	25,000	120,000	110,000
2360	Lacroix de Laville		1903			7/31/1961	14,000	F	Scoupe	10,000	0	40,000	66,000
2370	Lacroix de Laville		1903			8/27/1962	6,500	F	Thuysbaert	10,000	0	30,000	77,000
2402	Lancia	Epsilon	1913			9/23/1964	30,000	FS	Filipinetti	40,000	30,000	250,000	210,000
2410	Lancia	Lambda	1928	19315	9387	9/23/1964	8,000	FS	Filipinetti	40,000	50,000	150,000	220,000
2412	Lancia	Dilambda	1929	2757	67	11/19/1962	15,000	F	Nicholson	40,000	25,000	150,000	275,000
2430	La Licorne		1908		24370	9/10/1962	6,000	F	Malartre	20,000	25,000	50,000	83,000
2440	Lorraine Dietrich		1911			10/10/1962	10,000	F	Ruyer	17,000	18,000	45,000	115,000
2442	Lorraine Dietrich	EIC	1911	10123	10125	9/18/1962	15,000	F	Malartre	60,000	60,000	200,000	180,000
2450	Lorraine Dietrich	TVHH	1910	17121	170081	9/11/1962	8,000	F	Malartre	70,000	45,000	160,000	170,000
2460	Lorraine Dietrich	FRHF4	1913	15824	15808	10/31/1962	9,500	F	Mette	25,000	15,000	80,000	105,000
2464	Lorraine Dietrich	B6	1929	121838	132008	6/4/1961	800	F	Jund Vendenheim	35,000	20,000	60,000	100,000
2470	Lotus	18	1961	913	1191	7/10/1967	14,000	FS	Siffert	35,000	35,000	170,000	245,000
2472	Lotus	24	1962	949	1233	7/10/1967	10,000	FS	Siffert	45,000	30,000	350,000	275,000
2478	Lotus	33	1964	R9		7/10/1967	16,000	FS	Siffert	70,000	35,000	500,000	310,000
2490	MAF	5/14PS	1914	890	920	10/31/1962	3,000	FS	Hüni	30,000	15,000	100,000	100,000
2510	Maserati	26B	1926	2029	2029	4/3/1963	6,000	FS	Eckert	180,000	80,000	450,000	720,000
2514	Maserati	8CM	1933	3010	3010	1/13/1966	40,500	F	Pozzoli	220,000	80,000	700,000	1,270,000
2518	Maserati	4CM	1936	1526	3	1/9/1963	2,500	FS	Eckert	140,000	35,000	550,000	530,000
2522	Maserati	4CL	1939	1578	1571	1/9/1963	2,500	FS	Eckert	120,000	55,000	450,000	550,000
2526	Maserati	4CL	1938			1/13/1966	13,500	F	Pozzoli	80,000	20,000	400,000	220,000
2552	Maserati	250F	1958	2530	2530	3/15/1966	30,000	FS	Martinelli	260,000	120,000	500,000	720,000
2570	Maserati	300S	1955	3065	35	11/7/1964	5,000	FS	Centro Sud	150,000	100,000	1,200,000	1,100,000
2580	Maserati	4CLT	1948			9/24/1962	400,000	Lit	Farina	170,000	80,000	600,000	770,000
2595	Mathis	SB	1923	35130	37733	5/15/1961	500	F	Krafft	6,000	5,000	25,000	33,000
2610	Maurer-Union	18	1901		8	6/5/1968	27,500	DM	Interport	70,000	35,000	100,000	177,000
2620	Maybach	SW38	1936	1721	11933	8/28/1962	2,500	F	Sipp	10,000	10,000	250,000	235,000
2622	Maybach	SW38	1937	1800	11236	8/24/1964	6,000	FS	Dursteler	40,000	15,000	500,000	400,000
2624	Maybach	SW38	1937	1820	11278	9/4/1961	1,000	DM	Krefeld	20,000	20,000	250,000	235,000
2636	Maybach	SW38	1937	1876	11376	8/24/1964	4,000	FS	Dursteler	20,000	15,000	250,000	220,000
2640	Maybach	DS8	1934	1259	12058	3/16/1967	25,000	FS	Dursteler	200,000	80,000	1,000,000	1,350,000
2642	Maybach	DS8	1930	1277	12077	5/16/1967	1,800	FS	Eckert	70,000	35,000	800,000	930,000
2644	Maybach	DS8	1930	1317	12114	10/8/1962	9,000	F	Truninger	50,000	35,000	800,000	780,000
2680	Menier		1895		430	5/3/1965	Unknown		Libert	100,000	70,000	500,000	550,000

REF #	Marque	Type	Year	Chassis #	Engine #	Purchased	Bought for	Currency	Purchased from	Hervé Poulain (F)	Chappelon (F)	Huet (F)	Christie's (F)
2700	Mercedes	28/32 PS	1905		12526	7/13/1965	4,000	FS	Eckert	90,000	120,000	400,000	825,000
2710	Mercedes	39/75 PS	1907	4642	7380	3/10/1965	20,000	FS	Eckert	150,000	175,000	1,000,000	1,350,000
2712	Mercedes	14/30 PS	1909	850	12651	6/21/1971	12,000	FS	Filipinetti	120,000	80,000	250,000	310,000
2720	Mercedes-Benz	K	1926	1435		3/16/1967	25,000	FS	Dursteler	70,000	40,000	350,000	440,000
2730	Mercedes-Benz	K	1929	19506	35421	1/6/1966	16,200	F	Pozzoli	110,000	70,000	300,000	420,000
2740	Mercedes		1924	26992	55288	9/11/1964	500	Pound	Johnson	160,000	140,000	450,000	1,000,000
2742	Mercedes	T400	1925	20089	39593	6/28/1968	20,000	DM	Interport	90,000	60,000	400,000	340,000
2750	Mercedes-Benz	38/250SS	1929	36238	72344	1/1/1963	500	Pound	Simmons	150,000	100,000	1,300,000	2,000,000
2760	Mercedes	6/25/40	1923			5/31/1967	40,000	DM	Intrac	80,000	45,000	200,000	300,000
2770	Mercedes-Benz	SS	1928	3621772334	72334	7/26/1967	2,750	Pound	King	180,000	75,000	1,200,000	1,600,000
2780	Mercedes-Benz	SSK				5/31/1967	50,000	DM	Intrac	250,000	150,000	0	0
2781	Mercedes-Benz	SSK	1928		72304	8/25/1972	70,000	FS	Eckert	250,000	140,000	800,000	3,300,000
2800	Mercedes-Benz	380K	1933	103362	103362	8/25/1964	6,000	FS	Eckert	70,000	35,000	350,000	420,000
2810	Mercedes-Benz	500K	1934		123744	8/28/1962	4,000	FS	Sipp	20,000	16,000	300,000	500,000
2820	Mercedes-Benz	170H	1936	137546	137546	6/24/1964	1,200	F	Pierrard	10,000	10,000	150,000	55,000
2830	Mercedes-Benz	170V	1936	188530	188530	11/18/1964	800	FS	Eckert	10,000	8,000	150,000	90,000
2840	Mercedes-Benz	320	1938	408101	101121	1/6/1966	2,700	F	Pozzoli	20,000	7,000	180,000	140,000
2850	Mercedes-Benz	500K	1936	113673/20	408360	8/17/1959	3,500	F	Devavrin	230,000	45,000	600,000	1,200,000
2860	Mercedes-benz	540K	1938	169402	169402	8/19/1964	6,000	FS	Eckert	220,000	75,000	1,200,000	2,100,000
2862	Mercedes-Benz	540K	1936	130904	130904	8/6/1963	400	Pound	Dale Londres	150,000	50,000	500,000	690,000
2864	Mercedes-Benz	540K	1937	169395	169395	3/16/1967	27,000	FS	Performance car	230,000	65,000	800,000	950,000
2870	Mercedes-Benz	290	1937	141748	141748		5,000	FS	Hüni	60,000	35,000	300,000	135,000
2880	Mercedes-Benz	770K	1938	16495	189779	5/31/1961	3,500	F	Merklen	60,000	60,000	800,000	940,000
2884	Mercedes-Benz	770K	1938	189783	189783	5/18/1967	17,000	FS	Bendel	280,000	120,000	1,500,000	1,760,000
2900	Mercedes-Benz	W125	1937	166372	166368	3/8/1966	12,000	FS	Daimler	500,000	240,000	3,500,000	5,500,000
2910	Mercedes-Benz	W154	1939			5/6/1965	20,000	FS	Eckert	450,000	250,000	4,000,000	4,200,000
2912	Mercedes-Benz	W154	1939	189436	189439	3/8/1966	14,000	FS	Daimler	450,000	160,000	4,000,000	4,200,000
2930	Mercedes-benz	300S				8/24/1964	6,000	FS	Hüni	60,000	50,000	250,000	440,000
2939	Mercedes-Benz	300SL	1955	550017	550022		0		Schlumpf	130,000	130,000	350,000	440,000
2940	Mercedes-Benz	300SLR	1955	5.55		3/8/1966	15,000	FS	Daimler	500,000	300,000	5,000,000	4,440,000
2950	Mercedes-Benz	300SC	1956	188014	199980	7/31/1964	8,000	FS	Burrus	60,000	0	250,000	245,000
3020	Minerva	GS	1928			5/31/1967	15,000	DM	Intrac	120,000	60,000	350,000	385,000
3022	Minerva	AN	1928	67341	67368	7/10/1967	7,500	FS	Siffert	25,000	13,000	120,000	85,000
3032	Monet-Goyon	VM	1924	303		10/5/1962	3,000	F	Mette	10,000	10,000	20,000	31,000
3034	Monet-Goyon	VM	1925	417-3		9/14/1964	2,000	F	Ruyer	10,000	10,000	20,000	31,000
3050	Mors	N	1904	19067	19067	9/27/1962	12,000	F	Cibié	150,000	50,000	200,000	240,000
3052	Mors	SSS	1923/24	127-191		5/27/1962	4,500	F	Doumerc	25,000	15,000	60,000	88,000
3060	Ner-A-Car		1921	518PHT 176032	21504	4/30/1963	20	Pound	Ellis	3,000	3,000	10,000	18,000
3062	Ner-A-Car		1921	610337PB3562		4/30/1963	50	Pound	Ellis	3,500	3,000	10,000	18,000
3070	O.M.	667	1931	665088	665088	4/19/1963	3,000	FS	Eckert	70,000	45,000	250,000	230,000
3108	Panhard		1892		331	10/13/1971	90,000	F	Bruat	130,000	90,000	400,000	530,000
3110	Panhard	A1	1897	169	1221	10/19/1964	42,000	F	Barré	130,000	60,000	280,000	250,000
3112	Panhard	A2	1900	1573	1573	8/24/1964	7,000	FS	Dursteler	90,000	50,000	200,000	255,000
3114	Panhard		1908			9/18/1962	15,000	F	Malartre	130,000	70,000	180,000	180,000
3116	Panhard		1908		1035	1/6/1966	108,000	F	Pozzoli	350,000	150,000	1,200,000	2,600,000
3130	Panhard	U1	1906	6628	12159	7/31/1961	2,200	F	Sipp	50,000	55,000	200,000	137,000
3132	Panhard	X8	1911	13798	21226	7/31/1961	14,000	F	Scoupe	140,000	75,000	250,000	290,000
3134	Panhard	X12	1912	13570	13566	7/31/1961	14,000	F	Scoupe	130,000	70,000	250,000	245,000
3140	Panhard	X19		36963		11/16/1962	2,500	F	Spira	7,000	5,000	50,000	0
3150	Panhard	X26	1915	7950	55184	11/7/1962	10,000	F	Raffaelli	90,000	70,000	350,000	485,000
3160	Panhard	X29	1920	8156	52729	8/28/1962	6,800	F	Sipp	20,000	15,000	120,000	220,000
3170	Panhard				37236	7/24/1961	6,000	F	Busselet	10,000	6,000	50,000	44,000
3200	Pegaso	Z102BS	1952	01021530127		4/10/1964	40,000	PES	Vina	25,000	25,000	100,000	132,000

REF #	Marque	Type	Year	Chassis #	Engine #	Purchased	Bought for	Currency	Purchased from	Hervé Poulain (F)	Chappelon (F)	Huet (F)	Christie's (F)
3210	Peugeot		1890		608	12/24/1962	26,000	F	Lacroix	150,000	50,000	200,000	440,000
3211	Peugeot	AR				2/7/1973	20,000	F	Barré	90,000	35,000	250,000	155,000
3212	Peugeot	T3	1892		260	10/20/1965	12,500	F	Varin	110,000	70,000	300,000	320,000
3214	Peugeot		1895		348	6/7/1963	20,000	F	Lefranc	100,000	60,000	300,000	250,000
3218	Peugeot	T58	1900	3300	2877	5/23/1972	40,000	F	Mansuy	50,000	30,000	200,000	198,000
3220	Peugeot		1905			8/28/1962	13,400	F	Sipp	15,000	15,000	40,000	72,000
3230	Peugeot	8CV	1898		1748	6/18/1965	20,000	F	Palissy Garage	50,000	35,000	200,000	170,000
3240	Peugeot	T58	1903		21271	8/20/1964	16,000	F	Renfer	20,000	15,000	180,000	150,000
3245	Peugeot	T78A	1906	7029	7029	9/10/1962	15,000	F	Malartre	70,000	55,000	150,000	150,000
3250	Peugeot	T65	1904		1175	11/16/1962	4,000	F	Loyens	40,000	30,000	150,000	150,000
3252	Peugeot	T53	1903		06943	1/6/1964	16,000	F	Fétick	8,000	8,000	50,000	72,000
3260	Peugeot	BB				8/24/1966	Unknown		Sceaux	6,000	0	0	0
3261	Peugeot	BB				10/31/1962	2,500	F	Mette	3,000	3,000	20,000	22,000
3262	Peugeot	BB		12878		9/17/1961	1,000	F	Malartre	8,000	10,000	20,000	33,000
3263	Peugeot	BB		11393		1/23/1962	1,000	F	Raizon	2,000	2,000	20,000	22,000
3264	Peugeot	BB	1913	10591		7/31/1961	1,000	F	Sac	26,000	25,000	50,000	61,000
3265	Peugeot	BB	1915	11284		8/28/1962	4,000	F	Sac	26,000	25,000	70,000	77,000
3266	Peugeot	BB	1913	10602		3/1/1964	1,000	Dollar	Shakespeare	27,000	35,000	50,000	66,000
3267	Peugeot	BB	1913	11510		7/31/1961	1,700	F	Sipp	30,000	35,000	70,000	66,000
3275	Peugeot	146	1913/14	19506		3/16/1967	20,000	FS	Dursteler	50,000	50,000	50,000	132,000
3280	Peugeot	T161	1921	2135	2174	5/3/1965	2,000	F	Liber	15,000	15,000	60,000	61,000
3281	Peugeot	T161				8/27/1962	500	F	Doumerc	15,000	10,000	55,000	55,000
3284	Peugeot	T172				3/1/1966	Unknown		Mulhouse	1,000	2,500	20,000	20,000
3285	Peugeot	174SS				3/27/1962	2,000	F	Clog	20,000	18,000	55,000	55,000
3286	Peugeot	174SS				1/13/1966	10,800	F	Pozzoli	70,000	70,000	170,000	170,000
3300	Philos	8CV	1914		12390	8/28/1962	5,800	F	Sipp	25,000	25,000	105,000	105,000
3310	Piccard Pictet		1912	630	630	5/12/1965	20,000	F	Pozzoli	60,000	50,000	0	187,000
3330	Piccolo		1908			5/31/1961	10,000	F	Merkelen	45,000	35,000	0	138,000
3331	Piccolo		1906	747		6/5/1968	20,000	DM	Interport	30,000	35,000	0	110,000
3336	Piccolo					7/4/1957	0		Weill	12,000	0	0	0
3340	Piccolo		1907	946		6/16/1964	3,000	DM	Stotz	30,000	30,000	0	120,000
3350	Pilian	4D	1911	4045	4095	7/31/1961	5,000	F	Giovannoli	50,000	35,000	0	110,000
3354	Pilian	4D	1910			7/31/1961	2,250	F	Sac	50,000	45,000	0	150,000
3358	Porsche	908	1968	908013			0			0	65,000	0	0
3360	Ravel	12CV	1927	121	127	8/28/1962	3,600	F	Sipp	8,000	0	0	60,000
3405	Renault		1899			9/25/1962	20,000	F	Thuysbaert	70,000	35,000	0	300,000
3406	Renault	C	1900		3212	6/7/1963	20,000	F	Lefranc	50,000	30,000	0	130,000
3420	Renault	10CV	1904/05			10/22/1962	6,000	F	Sipp	50,000	35,000	0	105,000
3426	Renault	AX	1911			10/5/1962	5,000	F	Mette	35,000	20,000	0	75,000
3430	Renault	T	1901	3136	119	8/24/1964	9,000	FS	Schaffner	50,000	50,000	0	138,000
3435	Renault	AG1	1907			9/7/1962	3,600	F	Morel	30,000	30,000	0	85,000
3436	Renault	AX	1912			8/27/1962	12,500	F	Doumerc	40,000	30,000	0	85,000
3440	Renault	AX	1908			7/31/1961	7,000	F	Garage de l'avenue	35,000	35,000	0	90,000
3441	Renault	AX				4/13/1964	9,500	F	Montant	35,000	30,000	0	82,000
3444	Renault	AG1	1907			9/11/1962	5,000	F	Malartre	55,000	40,000	0	101,000
3460	Renault	AG1	1908			11/16/1961	9,000	F	Djaniguian	50,000	30,000	200,000	170,000
3470	Renault	55EV	1921			10/5/1962	5,000	F	Mette	55,000	35,000	100,000	90,000
3480	Renault	VB	1914			9/17/1962	8,500	F	Malartre	65,000	60,000	200,000	175,000
3482	Renault	40CV	1925			11/19/1962	15,230	F	Montant	170,000	100,000	500,000	430,000
3500	Rhéde		1899			5/10/1965	15,000	F	Pozzoli	30,000	20,000	130,000	121,000
3510	Georges Richard	Victoria	1897		229	7/31/1961	4,000	F	Sipp	60,000	45,000	180,000	265,000
3514	Georges Richard	Vedrine	1900	316/456		8/20/1964	15,000	F	Renfer	40,000	25,000	100,000	180,000
3518	Georges Richard		1901	109E		6/2/1964	11,500	F	Fétick	40,000	25,000	90,000	137,000
3530	Riley	1.5 Litre				4/19/1963	500	FS	Eckert	5,000	4,000	40,000	7,000
3540	Ripert		1901			7/31/1961	3,000	F	Sac	80,000	40,000	250,000	225,000
3550	Rochet					7/3/1961	0		Christen	16,000	0	0	0
3554	Rochet					1/23/1962	1,500	F	Djaniguian	5,000	3,000	25,000	55,000
3560	Rochet-Schneider		1912			9/19/1962	8,000	F	Malartre	12,000	6,000	40,000	61,000
3562	Rochet-Schneider	18CV	1924	25228		9/17/1962	3,000	F	Malartre	15,000	15,000	70,000	65,000
3564	Rochet-Schneider		1912	11964		8/27/1962	13,500	F	Doumerc	35,000	30,000	130,000	127,000
3610	Rolls-Royce	Silver Ghost	1912	2076		9/23/1964	40,000	FS	Filipinetti	120,000	200,000	300,000	450,000
3612	Rolls-Royce	Silver Ghost	1922	161DV	E3849	4/30/1963	95	Pound	Ellis	70,000	30,000	150,000	155,000
3614	Rolls-Royce	Silver Ghost	1921	68JG		8/24/1964	10,000	FS	Dursteler	220,000	180,000	600,000	575,000
3616	Rolls-Royce	Silver Ghost	1925	129EM	18761	8/24/1964	20,000	FS	Schaffner	250,000	200,000	200,000	465,000
3630	Rolls-Royce	20/25 HP	1929	GXC-69	W7F	11/3/1962	4,500	FS	Douville	50,000	20,000	70,000	160,000
3632	Rolls-Royce	20/25 HP	1934		GAE26	11/23/1961	1,500	F	Trivier	20,000	30,000	70,000	61,000

REF #	Marque	Type	Year	Chassis #	Engine #	Purchased	Bought for	Currency	Purchased from	Hervé Poulain (F)	Chappelon (F)	Huet (F)	Christie's (F)
3633	Rolls-Royce	20 HP	1925	48	G1369	12/1/1960	4,000	F	Vilmorin	60,000	40,000	120,000	110,000
3634	Rolls-Royce					7/31/1961	1,600	F	Sipp	20,000	20,000	0	180,000
3640	Rolls-Royce	Phantom I	1929	81WR	GX85	7/31/1961	1,600	F	Sipp	220,000	180,000	400,000	345,000
3650	Rolls-Royce	Phantom II	1929			4/5/1967	25,000	FS	Eckert	170,000	130,000	450,000	380,000
3652	Rolls-Royce	Phantom II	1930	161GY	LX25	7/31/1961	4,500	F	Raffaelli	70,000	40,000	400,000	400,000
3654	Rolls-Royce	Phantom II	1930	73GN	RS55	10/16/1962	11,500	F	Bolloré	130,000	90,000	400,000	380,000
3660	Rolls-Royce	Phantom III	1936	3BV140	748C	9/18/1964	10,000	F	Ote Orssich	60,000	60,000	200,000	245,000
3662	Rolls-Royce	Phantom III	1937	7DL176	272	3/23/1959	2,500	F	Malard	70,000	40,000	250,000	230,000
3664	Rolls-Royce	Phantom III	1938	3AZ196	3AZ196	1/25/1961	40,000	F	Sipp	90,000	45,000	200,000	200,000
3666	Rolls-Royce	Phantom III			DS82	10/30/1962	1,500	FS	Tognazzo	100,000	65,000	200,000	255,000
3700	Georges Roy					8/27/1962	2,500	F	Thuysbaert	6,000	4,500	30,000	46,000
3710	Sage		1904/05		A1505	5/3/1965	26,000	F	Liber	100,000	120,000	700,000	650,000
3712							0			0	3,000	0	0
3720	Salmson	GSS	1926	21121	21121	7/31/1961	2,000	F	Sipp	30,000	30,000	130,000	165,000
3740	Théophile Schneider				13942	9/17/1962	4,000	F	Malartre	10,000	5,500	40,000	33,000
3742	Théophile Schneider			11732		10/31/1962	6,000	F	Mette	5,000	3,000	20,000	33,000
3760	Scott		1921/25		316673	5/16/1963	195	Pound	Ellis	12,000	6,000	40,000	45,000
3770	Sénéchal	77-109	1924	6306	77109	9/11/1962	2,250	F	Raizon	25,000	20,000	90,000	88,000
3800	Serpollet	Circuit du Nord	1903			11/26/1966	125,000	F	Liber	500,000	250,000	1,500,000	1,700,000
3802	Serpollet	Gardner	1902			2/23/1965	63,000	F	Forest	250,000	200,000	800,000	550,000
3804	Serpollet	Gardner	1900/01			8/28/1962	30,000	F	Sac	250,000	200,000	450,000	400,000
3806	Serpollet		1900			4/13/1964	60,000	F	Sipp	250,000	150,000	500,000	450,000
3807	Serpollet	Gardner	1904			1/28/1969	100,000	F	Liber	250,000	150,000	500,000	500,000
3860	Sizaire Naudin	10CV	1908		3007	1/15/1963	4,500	F	Goldhann	65,000	25,000	150,000	140,000
3870	Soncin		1901		122		6,000	F	Barré	10,000	7,500	25,000	71,000
3886	Steyr	220	1935		4417925	9/2/1963	700	DM	Johan	15,000	10,000	70,000	48,000
3890	Sunbeam	16HP	1921	2253CB	2543CB	5/16/1963	150	Pound	Ellis	25,000	15,000	130,000	88,000
3900	Talbot	London	1933	35022	95AV37	4/19/1963	3,000	FS	Eckert	15,000	5,000	0	0
3910	Talbot	500	1948		44	8/1/1959	3,500	F	Girardot	250,000	140,000	800,000	880,000
3912	Talbot	500	1948			1/6/1966	40,500	F	Pozzoli	250,000	100,000	800,000	880,000
3950	Tatra	T87	1937	70006	870801	7/31/1961	800	F	Sipp	10,000	10,000	40,000	40,000
3960	Turicum	DI	1911			9/17/1962	7,000	F	Malartre	40,000	25,000	100,000	110,000
3970	Vermorel	T2	1899	21	21	7/31/1961	14,000	F	Scoupe	100,000	60,000	200,000	185,000
3980	Violet-Bogey	A	1914	598		9/25/1962	6,000	F	Vincent	20,000	15,000	55,000	72,000
4000	Voisin	C11	1927	18383	10707	1/25/1963	3,000	F	Vignardet	40,000	20,000	100,000	70,000
4010	Voisin	C14	1930	28365	27734	6/18/1957	1,500	F	Hartzer	40,000	25,000	80,000	80,000
4020	Voisin	C28	1936	53042	53026	8/23/1962	4,000	F	Rey	60,000	40,000	120,000	200,000
4050	Le Zèbre	A	1909	7226	657	6/17/1957	4,500	F	Kaufmann	34,000	25,000	55,000	75,000
4052	Le Zèbre	A	1908	501		7/31/1961	2,500	F	Sac	25,000	20,000	65,000	75,000
4054	Le Zèbre	A	1909/10	491	491	5/5/1962	6,500	F	Bonnin	35,000	25,000	65,000	75,000
4060	Le Zèbre	C	1912		422		6,000	F	Spira	15,000	20,000	55,000	72,000
4062	Le Zèbre	C4	1913	4593	308	7/31/1961	4,500	F	Garage de l'avenue	15,000	15,000	60,000	82,000
4064	Le Zèbre	C4	1914	3372	5177	10/5/1962	5,000	F	Mette	15,000	15,000	50,000	77,000
4100	Zedel	C1	1911	1410	24304	9/19/1962	18,000	F	Malartre	20,000	20,000	100,000	95,000
4102	Zedel	CA	1910		19245	8/27/1962	8,000	F	Thuysbaert	12,000	12,000	50,000	70,000

MINISTERE DE LA CULTURE ET DE LA COMMUNICATION

Décret du 14 avril 1978 portant classement parmi les monuments historiques de véhicules automobiles.

Par décret en date du 14 avril 1978, les véhicules automobiles figurant sur la liste annexée (1) au présent décret sont classés parmi les monuments historiques.

(1) La liste annexée pourra être consultée au ministère de la culture et de la communication (direction de l'architecture, sous-direction des monuments historiques), 3, rue de Valois, 75001 Paris, et à la préfecture du Haut-Rhin, 68000 Colmar.

Budget de l'Agence financière de bassin Rhône-Méditerranée-Corse.

For tactical reasons the collection was designated French patrimony.
(Op de Weegh archives)

PROJET No. 2 - 24 personnes employées

MUSEEE SCHLUMPF

I./ PROJECTIONS D'ENTREES

Nombre de visiteurs par année	Prix d'entrée (net)		
	F. 10	F. 15	F. 20
200.000	2.000.000	3.000.000	4.000.000
300.000	3.000.000	4.500.000	6.000.000
400.000	4.000.000	6.000.000	8.000.000
500.000	5.000.000	7.500.000	10.000.000
600.000	6.000.000	9.000.000	12.000.000
700.000	7.000.000	10.500.000	14.000.000

Entrance prices and revenues, sometime in the past.
(Op de Weegh archives)

List of the Malmerspach collection

Below is a list of all vehicles that Fritz and Hans Schlumpf owned in the Malmerspach collection at the time of the takeover by the workers. To give a good idea of the prices Fritz and Hans paid for these vehicles, we provide the dates of purchase and the amounts. Moreover, in the last columns you will see the various appraisal values according to Christie's and Christian Huet (hired by Fritz Schlumpf) and Poulain and Chappelon (on behalf of the French government).

We have made the list as complete as possible on the basis of documentation at our disposal, and therefore assume that it is correct. Yet, we cannot guarantee this. Modifications reserved.

REF#	Marque	Type	Year	Chassis #	Engine #	Purchased	Bought for	Currency	Purchased from	Hervé Poulain (F)	Chappelon (F)	Huet (F)
71	Bugatti	T40	1927	40436	304	8/28/1962	4,000	F	Sac	55,000	250,000	210,000
72	Bugatti	T40	1927	40485	714	3/1/1964	2,500	Dollar	Shakespeare	20,000	200,000	190,000
77	Bugatti	T40	1929	40618		8/24/1964	5,000	FS	Dursteler	30,000	150,000	210,000
80	Bugatti	T40A	1931	40902	4	3/1/1964	2,500	Dollar	Shakespeare	60,000	0	220,000
117	Bugatti	T44	1931	441322	1047	3/1/1964	2,500	Dollar	Shakespeare	60,000	200,000	250,000
220	Bugatti	T57	1934	57168	41	8/24/1964	5,000	FS	Shakespeare	50,000	300,000	255,000
221	Bugatti	T57	1934	57224	112	4/19/1963	2,000	FS	Eckert	30,000	300,000	265,000
222	Bugatti	T57	1935	57338	237	3/1/1964	2,500	Dollar	Shakespeare	60,000	300,000	245,000
223	Bugatti	T57	1935	57327	233	4/8/1963	4,000	F	Daniel	65,000	500,000	265,000
	Bugatti	T57	1936	57377	278		Unknown			0	0	0
224	Bugatti	T57	1935	57297	151	1/29/1963	6,000	F	Spira	40,000	400,000	245,000
234	Bugatti	T57	1937	57507	14C	3/1/1964	2,500	Dollar	Shakespeare	55,000	450,000	310,000
	Bugatti	T57	1937	57535	375	3/1/1964	Unknown		Shakespeare	0	0	0
235	Bugatti	T57	1937	57546	400	3/1/1964	2,500	Dollar	Shakespeare	30,000	250,000	221,000
236	Bugatti	T57C	1938	57728	48C	7/1/1961	1,600	F	Sipp	60,000	300,000	300,000
	Bugatti						Unknown			0	0	220,000
	Bugatti						Unknown			0	0	530,000
	Bugatti						Unknown			0	0	8,000
	Alfa Romeo	6C2300	1937	814047	823106	1/9/1963	1,500	FS	Eckert	180,000	200,000	100,000
1140	Auto Union	W25	1937	180223	180231	7/31/1961	2,300	F	Sipp	25,000	90,000	93,000
1190	Bédélia					1/23/1962	3,500	F	Raizon	8,000	20,000	22,000
1192	Bédélia					8/27/1962	3,500	F	Doumerc	8,000	25,000	35,000
1330	Bucciali					5/27/1964	15,000	F	Mortarini	10,000	30,000	100,000
1430	Cord	812	1937	32122		10/8/1962	800	FS	Truninger	25,000	40,000	110,000
1432	Cord	812	1935	21315		6/7/1961	3,000	F	Lepage	10,000	40,000	110,000
1440	Cottin-Desgouttes	T		50102		8/28/1962	2,600	F	Sipp	12,000	40,000	39,000
1550	Darmont	Morgan				9/17/1962	1,500	F	Malartre	7,000	30,000	33,000
1552	Darmont	Special				8/27/1962	500	F	Doumerc	8,000	35,000	33,000
1660	De Dion Bouton	IW		11223		8/28/1962	2,400	F	Sipp	30,000	30,000	39,000
1686	Delage	CO		7216		2/23/1965	2,000	F	Forest	7,000	30,000	42,000
1688	Delage	BK	1918			9/17/1962	3,500	F	Malartre	20,000	40,000	44,000
1690	Delage	S8S	1932	36025		8/28/1962	3,600	F	Sipp	30,000	150,000	175,000
1694	Delage					7/1/1966	540	F	Wittelsheim	5,000	15,000	28,000
1698	Delage	D63L	1948	880100		2/6/1961	750	F	Fiener	17,000	40,000	44,000
1724	Delage	T87	1924			3/21/1963	4,000	F	Barré	12,000	0	61,000
1861	Fiat	2800			16		0		Gordini	1,000	20,000	22,000
1874	Ford	T				2/9/1965	1,000	F	Bugatti	1,000	15,000	9,000
1876	Ford	T				10/31/1962	4,000	F	Mette	3,500	15,000	24,000
1878	Ford	Montier				7/31/1961	2,100	F	Sipp	30,000	55,000	78,000
2290	Georges-Irat	T4A	1926	2515	10416	2/23/1965	2,000	F	Forest	25,000	50,000	42,000
2380	Laffly					9/10/1963	1,200	F	Mallebay	5,000	15,000	55,000
2414	Lancia	Astura				10/8/1962	500	FS	Truninger	4,000	40,000	32,000
2416	Lancia					4/19/1963	500	FS	Eckert	1,000	10,000	18,000
2420	Laurin-Clément		1924	2386	7289	1/15/1963	2,000	F	Heger	6,000	15,000	32,000
2452	Lorraine-Dietrich	FHB	1914	12411		10/25/1963	3,000	F	Koville	10,000	40,000	50,000
2650	Maybach	Zeppelin		1336		1/6/1966	9,000	F	Pozzoli	10,000	200,000	385,000
2790	Mercedes-Benz	290				3/26/1963	800	DM	Kaliwerke	0	30,000	29,000
3024	Minerva		1932			10/30/1962	700	FS	Tognazzo	15,000	60,000	77,000

REF#	Marque	Type	Year	Chassis #	Engine #	Purchased	Bought for	Currency	Purchased from	Hervé Poulain (F)	Chappelon (F)	Huet (F)
3040	Montrace-Morgan		1922			9/11/1962	2,300	F	Raizon	4,000	15,000	42,000
3180	Panhard	SS				2/23/1965	2,000	F	Forest	12,000	35,000	0
3287	Peugeot	18CV				11/14/1962	1,800	F	Ruyer	10,000	0	22,000
3290	Peugeot	402DS	1937			9/17/1962	2,500	F	Malartre	15,000	0	66,000
3498	Renault	EA	1919			10/17/1961	600	F	Chaumeau	3,500	0	21,000
3850	Sizaire Frères	4RI	1926			9/23/1964	6,500	FS	Filipinetti	8,000	40,000	55,000
3880	Steyr	T2	1920			10/15/1962	1,600	F	Pfuger	12,000	45,000	40,000
3882	Steyr	T45	1929	45358		3/29/1963	850	F	Goldhann	2,000	25,000	29,000
3883	Steyr	T45	1929			3/29/1963	800	F	Goldhann	2,000	25,000	29,000
3884	Steyr	T45	1929	45719	45719	3/29/1963	850	F	Goldhann	2,000	25,000	29,000
3920	Talbot	15LB	1950			8/28/1962	1,600	F	Sipp	25,000	40,000	35,000
3965	Veritas						Unknown		Gordini	10,000	150,000	135,000

Recommandé + A. de R.

Mr. John. W. SHAKESPEARE
P.O. Box 10295
RIVIERA BEACH
     Florida U.S.A.

FS/ML

11th July 1963

Dear Sir,

  I really do not understand what happen with you and why you act on this manner.

  I wrote you June 14 und 17 and cabled you.

  Why do not you answer.

  Why do you not give me the date of expiration of the credit, so that I can open it.

  I wrote you each time very genteelly and I not will have difficulties with you.

  But you must acknowledge that you put my nerves on a hard trial.

  I will not give all our wriftings to a lawer that is not what I will with you, but why do you act so ?

  Eease anwer now immediatly, give me the date of expiration, than I open the credit and you can shipp than the cars, at first the Royale 41 and then the others as indicated on my letter of June 14.

  Awarting your immediat reply, I remain

     yours sincerely

    Fritz SCHLUMPF

This page & opposite: Correspondence between Fritz Schlumpf and John Shakespeare.
(Op de Weegh archives)

Mr. John W. SHAKESPEARE
514 S. Pine Street
CENTRALIA/ Illinois 62801

U.S.A.

Lettre recommandée + A.R.

FS/JW

24th. September 1963

Dear Sir,

My last letter dates from July 24th.

You did not answer.

Mr. Demade from the Bugatti works wrote you also concerning this 30 cars you sold me.

I do not understand your silence and think that you are still restoring and assembling my cars and that you shall be in the next days in the position to ship them.

I beg you therefore to indicate me the date of the shipment of the last car, so that I now can open the credits for you and that you can ship partially, it means one car after the other, as soon as you have finished the reassembling, or better 5 or 6 cars on the same steamer.

I am very impatient to have the cars.

Did you buy the 6 tires for the Royale and which is the price, so that I open also the credit for the tires.

Mr. Shaw saw you recently and I hope that you can now say me at which date you can surely ship the cars.

When do you think come over to France ?

Awaiting your immediat reply,

I remain, dear Sir,

yours sincerely,

FRITZ SCHLUMPF

Cité de l'Automobile, collection Schlumpf

A large portion of the Schlumpf collection can be admired in the museum in Mulhouse. We definitely recommend it to all automobile enthusiasts. The address is:

Cité de l'Automobile
15 rue de l'Épée
68100 Mulhouse
France

Above: 1912 Hispano-Suiza Type 13. (Photo collection Op de Weegh)

Above: 1923 Bugatti T32 Tank. (Photo collection Op de Weegh)

Below: Formula 1 race cars in today's museum in Mulhouse. (Photo collection Op de Weegh)

Below: 1929 Mercedes-Benz 250 SS. (Photo collection Op de Weegh)

Also from Veloce

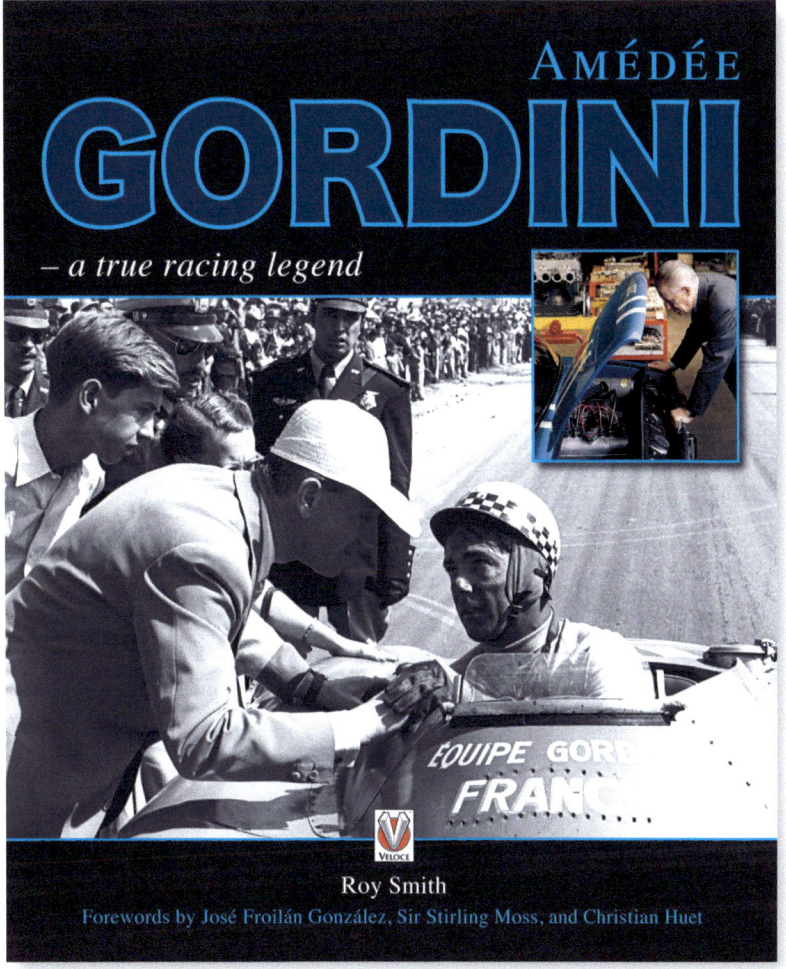

This is the story of a man, a team, and their life and times, as well as a complete record of all their achievements and failures. It logs the financial and personal cost of racing in the prewar and postwar periods. It tells of how the mighty car company Renault became involved with them in the late 1950s, and how Amédée Gordini became known throughout the world as one of the greatest engine tuners of his time.

ISBN: 978-1-845843-17-5

For more information and price details, visit our website at www.veloce.co.uk • email: info@veloce.co.uk
Tel: +44(0)1305 260068

Also from Veloce

Chronicles the development and racing career of a car regarded as the ultimate example of the purebred sports car of the 20th century and the epitome of functional beauty and extraordinary performance: the 1952 Mercedes-Benz 300 SL. Taking second place at its 1952 Mille Miglia debut, it went on to win every one of its races that season. Dramatic photos, vivid descriptions, and dramatic recollections from the drivers ensures this book will be a joy to read and enjoy for years to come.

ISBN: 978-1-845846-17-6

For more information and price details, visit our website at www.veloce.co.uk • email: info@veloce.co.uk
Tel: +44(0)1305 260068

Also from Veloce

A comprehensive, radical look at the history and development of the Type 57 Grand Prix Bugattis. New material challenges traditional beliefs about these historic cars, and rejects some long-standing conventions. Myths are explored and truths are revealed in a book celebrating all aspects of these remarkable cars and their creators.

ISBN: 978-1-845847-89-0

For more information and price details, visit our website at www.veloce.co.uk • email: info@veloce.co.uk
Tel: +44(0)1305 260068

Also from Veloce

The only book dedicated to the Type 46 & 50 Bugattis. Features over 200 period plates, many rare and previously unpublished, showing a galaxy of superb coachbuilt and standard bodies on T46 and T50 chassis as well as much mechanical detail. Regarded as THE standard reference to the Type 46 & 50.

ISBN: 978-1-845848-72-9

These post WW1 8-cylinder sporting touring cars were the most successful Bugatti models until the advent of the Type 57, and typify Bugatti style, design and innovative automobile engineering. Here is a thorough study of these great cars. Over 200 photos and drawings.

ISBN: 978-1-787110-98-4

The 4-cylinder Bugatti Type 40, sometimes unkindly referred to as 'Ettore's Morris Cowley,' nevertheless shared its fine engineering pedigree with all other Bugattis. Packed with mainly period photographs, illustrations and sales literature, the book also features the factory's individual chassis sales records.

ISBN: 978-1-787112-59-9

For more information and price details, visit our website at
www.veloce.co.uk • email: info@veloce.co.uk
Tel: +44(0)1305 260068

Index

Adatto 11, 136
Alfa Romeo
  412 126, 127
  6C1750 82, 126
  8C2300 126, 127
  8C2900 127

Basel 34
Braam Ruben, Jaap 11, 64, 70, 71, 75, 78, 95, 136
Bugatti
  T28 25
  T32 110, 122-124, 154
  T35 40, 110-112
  T35B 7, 8, 22, 24, 58, 110, 112
  T41 10, 29, 30, 47, 114, 115, 117
  T46 43, 136, 158
  T50 158
  T57 69, 70, 74, 76, 94, 95
  T57C 70, 71, 74, 75, 95, 134
  T57S 59, 95
  T57SC 95
  T251 33, 44-45

CFTD 34
Chappelon 44, 51, 140, 150
Cohen 34, 46, 48
Colmar 13, 74, 95
Conway, Hugh 63

de Rothschild, Nathaniel 34, 48
Dovaz, Michel 10, 13, 17, 74, 134
Dufilho, André 10, 27, 39, 72, 92-93, 136

Ferrari 250MM 118
France 7, 10, 11, 13, 15, 19, 20, 34, 37, 38, 46, 59, 68, 74, 78, 112, 134, 154

Glück 21
Gordini
  Amédée 32, 46, 122-124, 155
  T32 122, 124

Gulick, David 19, 64, 67, 136

Hottendorff, Kay 10, 36, 102, 134, 136
Huet, Christian 44, 45, 50, 62, 68-70, 75, 83, 84, 87, 91, 95, 136, 140, 150

Italy 69, 126, 134

Jansen, Kees 10, 136

Lancia Dilambda 4, 78, 80
Lansink 70, 78, 80, 136

Malmerspach 11, 26, 34, 38, 46, 48, 54, 63-65, 68, 69, 71, 75, 80, 83, 84, 86-88, 92, 95, 98, 101, 138, 150
Maserati
  4CM 102
Mercedes-Benz
  540K 61
  300SLR 58
  770K 43
  W154 106
Meyer, Martin 13, 37, 136
Mulhouse 7, 11, 13, 15, 17, 20-22, 27-30, 34-35, 37, 38, 43-46, 48, 62, 65, 68, 115, 118, 120, 123, 130, 140, 154
Mullin, Peter 11, 63-65, 70, 71, 86, 88, 92, 93, 95, 96, 136

Oxnard 63, 64, 70, 86, 88, 92

Panhard 37, 46, 52, 54, 59
Paris 16, 34, 62, 78, 83, 85-86, 122-123
Patenostre, Lionel 6, 7, 17, 20-22, 34, 111, 113, 136
Peugeot 36
Poulain-Loudner 44, 51
Prost, Jacques 13

Raffaelli, Mr 58, 59
Ripert, Mr 95

Schlumpf, Arlette 15, 17, 27, 37-39, 46, 48, 54, 62, 64, 69, 95, 130, 133
Schlumpf, Fritz 6-8, 11, 13, 15-17, 20-22, 26-28, 34, 36-39, 42-44, 46-48, 54, 58, 59, 62, 63, 68, 74, 95, 101, 111-113, 116, 122, 136, 140, 150, 152
Schlumpf, Hans 6, 13, 17, 20-22, 27, 34, 36, 43, 46, 48, 54, 90, 136, 140, 150
Schlumpf, Hermann 54
Shakespeare, John 19, 59, 63-65, 67, 74, 116, 152
Shaw, Bob 63

Tatra T87 53

van der Kroft, Adrian 70, 74, 76, 136
Vendiesse, Bruno 11, 64, 70, 78, 80, 95, 136

Wettolsheim 38, 69
Wheatcroft, Tom 15, 26, 42, 46, 136